# Japan's New Politics and the U.S.-Japan Alliance

COUNCIL *on*
FOREIGN
RELATIONS

July 2014

Sheila A. Smith

# Japan's New Politics and the U.S.-Japan Alliance

# Contents

*Acknowledgments  vii*

Introduction  1
*Seiken Kōtai* and the U.S.-Japan Alliance  3
The DPJ's Alliance Reform Agenda  8
The LDP's Alliance Reform Agenda  17
Reforming Japan's Policymaking  24
Implications for Alliance Management  30

*Endnotes  37*
*About the Author  48*
*Japan's Political Transition and the U.S.-Japan Alliance Roundtables  49*

# Acknowledgments

This report is the culmination of a three-year project undertaken by CFR's Japan program on Japan's Political Transition and the U.S.-Japan Alliance. Over the three years, a broad array of U.S. and Japanese policymakers and experts gathered to discuss the 2009 transition in government in Tokyo, the policy impact of a divided Diet, and the 2012 return of the Liberal Democratic Party to power. The project sought not only to understand the way this political transition in Japan affected policymaking, but also to explore the underlying linkages between Japan's domestic political change and alliance management. U.S. policymakers also helped us understand their perspective on the impact of Japanese elections on alliance management.

This project would not have been possible without the generous support provided by the U.S.-Japan Foundation and by the Japan Foundation Center for Global Partnership. I received tremendously valuable advice and insights from four leading Japanese political scientists: Nobumasa Akiyama, Masaaki Gabe, Toshihiro Nakayama, and Tomohito Shinoda. In Washington, DC, a series of Roundtable discussions were convened with experts on Japan's politics and policymaking from Japan and the United States. I want to thank in particular the senior officials from the U.S. and Japanese governments who shared their insights. A full list of the eighteen roundtables is provided at the end of the report. A special acknowledgment is extended to James M. Lindsay, CFR's director of studies, for his support of this project. I am grateful to Patricia Dorff for her excellent editorial oversight and to Eli Dvorkin for his assistance in the production of this report. Several interns of CFR's Japan program also provided support: Miyuki Naiki, Jennifer Ijichi, Ashley Sutton, Go Katayama, Yuko Shimada, Joelle Metcalfe, Yuki Yoshihisa, Andrew Morris, Jingtian Gong, and Tsuyoshi Takahashi.

This report reflects my analysis of Japan's change, and while I have benefitted greatly from the insights of our core experts and roundtable participants, I alone am responsible for the conclusions reached. However, I would have been unable to complete this report without the research assistance of my CFR research associate, Charles McClean. His own research on Japanese politics made him a terrific contributor to the project, and I am deeply grateful for his dedicated support throughout.

**Sheila A. Smith**
July 2014

# Introduction

Electoral reform in the early 1990s ended single-party dominance in Japan and promised an era of new politics in which political parties would alternate control of the government. In the two decades that followed, Japan's foreign and domestic policy priorities were subjected to greater scrutiny and debate as Japan, like so many other nations around the globe, sought to reorient itself in a new post–Cold War world. The U.S.-Japan alliance that anchored Japan's postwar foreign policy was not immune to these domestic political reforms. For half a century, the conservative Liberal Democratic Party (LDP) prided itself on managing the relationship with Washington. But its ouster in 2009 by the reformist Democratic Party of Japan (DPJ) led many to expect that even Japan's alliance with the United States would be subject to serious review.[1]

In the two decades since political alignments began to shift in Tokyo, new parties have come and gone. The dreaded divided Diet (*nejire kokkai*) that had confounded governance since 2007 was brought to an end when the LDP, led by Shinzo Abe, claimed victory in the 2013 upper house election. Although some of the dominant bureaucrats in Japan's foreign policy–making process continue to wield considerable influence, new currents of contention have emerged outside of government to contest some official choices. As important as these domestic pressures are, Japan must also contend with an unprecedented set of exogenous challenges to its foreign and security policy decisions. Popular anxiety coupled with more unsettled and contentious electoral politics will continue to complicate U.S.-Japan alliance policy.

The return to power of the LDP in late 2012 may seem to have restored the old order in Tokyo, but the changes wrought in the policymaking process cannot be undone.[2] Like the DPJ, today's LDP must contend with greater popular scrutiny of its policy ambitions and defend its ideas for reforming Japan against the clamor of new parties seeking to position themselves as agents of policy change. Japanese voters have now dealt punishing blows to both the LDP and DPJ, suggesting a growing sense of concern about the ability of Japan's politicians to solve their country's challenges. After twelve long years building Japan's second major party, the DPJ is now just one of many small parties in the opposition camp.[3] Nonetheless, the demand for governance reform remains, and the LDP will need to produce results if it is to maintain popular confidence.

The new politics in Tokyo have yet to prompt a debate over the value of the alliance to Japan. Political change in Japan has, however, shaped Tokyo's decision-making on the alliance. Moreover, the rapid turnover in cabinets and intensified legislative contention produced a stop-and-start effort at alliance decision-making. Ideas begun in one cabinet often had to wait for one or more cabinet shifts to be completed. Repeated crises, including the Great East Japan Earthquake and the outbreak of tensions with China over the Senkaku/Diaoyu Islands, highlighted the alliance role in Japan's security and focused attention on the need for better crisis management.

# *Seiken Kōtai* and the U.S.-Japan Alliance

The ambition of alternating parties in power, long part of democratic politics elsewhere, drove Japanese thinking about political reform for much of the 1990s. The introduction of single-member districts began a shift toward a two-party system that many hoped would stimulate greater policy competition. Just as Japan's politicians sought to enhance their role in policymaking, scandals rocked nearly every Japanese bureaucracy, revealing the misuse of funds and overly cozy relations between regulators and the interests they regulated, and popular confidence in Japan's bureaucrats diminished. Both the dominance of the LDP, Japan's major conservative party, and the influence of Japan's once highly regarded civil servants over policymaking eroded and the task of reforming Japan's governance began.

The call for a change in government, *seiken kōtai*, in the first decade of the twenty-first century revealed the hurdles that had faced opposition parties in Japan. The long-standing hold on government by the LDP and the structure of postwar politics meant that it was nearly impossible for a viable electoral contender to emerge to challenge single-party dominance. The demand for political reform, however, was palpable in Tokyo and even the LDP recognized it. The emergence of Junichiro Koizumi within the LDP as the advocate of political reform captured this need for change. But the LDP could not generate a consensus on change after Koizumi left office in 2006, which opened the way for the DPJ to claim the mantle of reform. *Seiken kōtai* became an end in itself. [4]

Japan's effort at political reform has been protracted. Electoral reform remains an unfinished process because Japan's combined system of single-member districts and proportional representation made it difficult for large parties to succeed and ensured the continued presence of smaller splinter parties. A variety of efforts to revamp the bureaucracy were considered, with varied results. It would take two decades for a rival political party to emerge that could challenge the grand old LDP.

This extended era of reform politics had three consequences for governing in Japan's parliamentary process. First, the dissolution of the LDP in 1993 created a kaleidoscope-like political realignment that continues today, more than twenty years later. Party loyalty was organized around personalities rather than policy identity, and even after a concerted effort to build a second major party in Japan that could challenge the LDP's dominance, the centrist DPJ seemed unable to hold itself together atop a coherent policy platform.

Second, the proliferation of parties in Japan produced the need for coalition government. No party, not even the LDP, could effectively govern alone. Even after winning majorities in the lower house, the two large parties, the LDP and the DPJ, needed the edge of smaller coalition partners to generate legislation. Today, the LDP seems unable to govern without the New Komeito Party, and past DPJ cabinets found it increasingly hard to govern as they had to constantly solicit the help of minor partners in the Diet.

Finally, Japan's voters grew increasingly disconnected from these ever-changing political parties, and more and more Japanese voters "floated"—i.e., changed which party they voted for in each election—making electoral outcomes more and more unpredictable. Thus in the lower house elections of 2005, 2009, and 2012, the margin of victory grew even as the party that won the election changed.[5] Japan's voters shifted their support from the LDP to the DPJ and back to the LDP, but this was not a cautious shift in loyalties. Voters repeatedly changed preferences in large numbers.

Surprisingly little of this new political energy was devoted to debating foreign policy, and few in Washington could anticipate the outcome of a transfer of government in Tokyo. Japanese foreign policy–making had always been subjected to Diet scrutiny, so when the DPJ secured a majority of seats in the 2007 upper house election, its influence over alliance policymaking increased. Although the new contention between the LDP and DPJ suggested that the contest over ideas drove policy debate, in large part these two parties were closer on Japan's foreign policy than their rhetoric might suggest. Rather than usher in a new era of policy competition over Japan's foreign policy goals, the new politics in Tokyo seemed only to slow decision-making.

Furthermore, U.S. policymakers had little experience with managing political transitions in Tokyo. The LDP had largely led the government, in majority or in coalition, since 1955, and although cabinets changed, they did so in a relatively predictable way. Prospective leaders in the conservative party were identified and groomed for cabinet positions.[6] The frequent turnover in Japan's cabinets made it difficult to anticipate or get to know Japan's foreign policy–makers, and with alternating parties in power it became increasingly difficult to build continuity in policy. In the 1990s, Japan had seven prime ministers, but the United States had only two presidents.[7] Only during the five-year tenure of Junichiro Koizumi as prime minister from 2001 to 2006 did the U.S. and Japanese governments achieve continuity in their alliance policy goals. In the three years after Koizumi, the LDP produced three prime ministers, who between them reshuffled the cabinet five times.[8] The DPJ did no better, changing its prime minister each year of its three years in office.[9] Each DPJ prime minister also felt it necessary to change his policy team, which meant a new foreign and defense minister every six months.[10] A divided Diet put particular pressure on governments after 2007. In upper house debate, censure motions were used to force cabinet reshuffles, and both the DPJ and the LDP as opposition parties used this tactic, to great advantage.[11]

The U.S.-Japan alliance was not immune to the popular call in Japan for policy reform. The leaders of Japan's new reformist party seemed willing to challenge past alliance management practices, especially on the basing of U.S. forces in Japan. Equally worrisome was the idea that the DPJ's first prime minister, Yukio Hatoyama, wanted to downgrade the relationship with the United States in favor of Japan's regional relations, especially with China.[12] Hatoyama ultimately failed to change Japan's basing strategy in Okinawa and was forced to leave office before his first year was up, leaving his party in disarray.[13] Nonetheless, the strained relations between this first DPJ government and the Barack Obama administration left a legacy that was difficult for succeeding DPJ governments to overcome, and left the DPJ vulnerable at home to criticism that the party was simply too inexperienced to manage Japan's foreign relations.

But Japan's reformers did not turn away from the alliance with Washington. Indeed, since Ichiro Ozawa and his followers left the LDP in 1993 determined to offer an alternative blueprint for Japan, there has been much debate—and anxiety—over how the end of the LDP's dominance in Japanese politics would shape the U.S.-Japan alliance.[14] Even as the DPJ came into office with a desire for change, its main focus was on how policy was made and implemented.[15] Many of the policies the Japanese government advocated on the alliance, including basing, nuclear deterrence, and regional security cooperation, had defined the U.S.-Japan security partnership through and beyond the Cold War. But the policies had not been fully shared with other political leaders or with the Japanese public for fear of criticism and opposition. The change in government in 2009, therefore, began a process of opening decision-making within the Japanese government to greater scrutiny and public evaluation. Japan's new politics challenged the implementation of alliance policy goals rather than the premises of security cooperation that underpinned the U.S.-Japan alliance.

Today, the United States and Japan must navigate an increasingly complex strategic environment, one in which the rise of China and the nuclearization of the Korean peninsula continue to draw alliance attention. Beyond the relief associated with the return of the LDP and the predictability that many in Washington assumed this would bring to alliance management, Tokyo and Washington continue to struggle with their different perceptions of risk and priorities for the alliance. What seems different today, however, is the appreciation for the shift in political expectations in Japan.

When once many Japanese looked forward to alternating parties in power, developing a two-party system that would offer voters serious policy debate, today there seems to be widespread dismissal of that notion. Furthermore, assumptions about what the cumulative legacy of Japan's new politics means for policymaking remain unexplored. The LDP campaigned in both recent elections on the notion that it would "restore Japan," but the reform agenda that the Abe cabinet puts forth is less about going back to the way things were and more about bringing a different vision of reform to Japan, especially regarding security policy.[16] The prime minister is determined to tackle his longtime ambition to normalize Japan's military and end the postwar constraints on its relations with its neighbors. But the Abe cabinet will not be immune to the pressures that plagued its predecessors. Though the call for policy reform is no less compelling, the ability of the Japanese government to change course remains in question.

The U.S.-Japan alliance is being shaped by the shifts in Japan's domestic politics, and the new politics of alternating parties in power—even if accomplished through coalition—require careful analysis and assessment for U.S. policymakers. This project began as an effort to understand how the advent of a DPJ government might shape the alliance, but today it has a broader purpose. Over three years, drawing on the insights of U.S. and Japanese policymakers, as well as of scholars of the alliance in both countries, an ongoing discussion about the impact of political change in Japan on alliance management revealed several ways in which alliance policymaking has changed since the end of single-party dominance in Japanese politics. The call for reform comes from not only liberals, but also conservatives, though their agendas for reform differ. Moreover, as its diplomacy in Asia comes under greater pressure, the Japanese government is finding its alliance choices increasingly under scrutiny. Popular anxiety about the continued efficacy of Japan's postwar foreign policy choices now shapes the politics in Tokyo over the alliance.

# The DPJ's Alliance Reform Agenda

Japanese liberals have long supported the restraint on military power embedded in Japan's postwar constitution. Just as some conservatives chafed against the postwar security bargain with the United States, liberals, too, sought to distance Tokyo from the subordinate relationship with Washington that seemed to accompany the alliance. Therefore, as new political parties emerged in the early 1990s, many politicians saw an opportunity for alliance reform following the end of the Cold War. The first coalition government to oust the LDP offered a glimpse of the alliance reform sought by many Japanese. Former prime minister Morihiro Hosokawa spoke for many of Japan's liberals when he wrote that the time had come for Japan to reap this peace dividend.[17] But Japan's conservatives also began to think anew about what the end of the Cold War meant for their postwar constitution, and Prime Ministers Koizumi and Abe would lead their party's debate over reinterpreting and ultimately revising Article 9 to allow Japan's own military to play a stronger role in national defense.[18]

But there were other reasons to focus on the U.S. military presence in Japan. The 1995 rape of a twelve-year-old schoolgirl in Okinawa prompted the outbreak of protest and citizen activism against the U.S. military bases there; these bases make up approximately three-fourths of the overall U.S. military presence in Japan. Here, too, Japan's domestic politics were an important ingredient in the management of the crisis. At the time, the LDP was in a coalition with the Japan Socialist Party (JSP), led by then prime minister Tomiichi Murayama. Murayama initially responded sympathetically to Okinawa governor Masahide Ota's demand to reduce the U.S. military presence on the island; the JSP supported the growing protest movement in opposition to the LDP's management of the issue.

The Okinawa protests prompted a renewed effort by the U.S. and Japanese governments to address the need to reduce the size of the

U.S. military presence there. The Special Action Committee on Okinawa overrode the regular consultative processes laid out in the Status of Forces Agreement (SOFA), and the problem of the U.S. bases in Okinawa was addressed by U.S. cabinet officials and ultimately the Japanese prime minister. The December 1996 decision to realign U.S. bases, including the closure of U.S. Marine Air Station Futenma, was also subject to broad opposition-party critique.[19] The relocation of Futenma was seen as an LDP policy with little or no support from other political parties in Tokyo. Yet the Diet passed a law in 1997 with cross-party support that changed the legal basis for managing protests against the use of base land.[20]

Several future leaders of the DPJ took aim at the U.S. military presence in Japan, arguing for greater accountability to Japanese citizens for the behavior of U.S. soldiers. The DPJ's president at the time of the 2009 lower house election, Yukio Hatoyama, called for a reduction of troops, and the party's secretary-general, Ichiro Ozawa, had long argued for a more independent Japanese foreign policy. The DPJ campaigned to revise the SOFA to make the United States more accountable under Japanese law and to reduce the concentration of U.S. bases in Okinawa.[21] But few in the DPJ openly questioned Japan's need for a security alliance with the United States.

In fact, Japan's new ruling party presented no new foreign policy ideas. In the study groups and manifesto developed by the DPJ, there was a striking absence of serious debate over Japan's foreign policy options. In the months leading up to the historic 2009 election, the manifesto had to be amended and some foreign policy points added to flesh out the DPJ's governing agenda.[22] Only one foreign policy priority was clearly articulated: the DPJ's stance on North Korea. But the DPJ did not diverge from the existing Japanese government approach. Missile tests by Pyongyang in 2006 and 2009, coupled with a lack of progress in bilateral efforts on abducted Japanese citizens, meant that there was little room for diverging from the policy developed by the LDP.

Once in office, the DPJ focused on three long-standing complaints about the LDP's running of the alliance: the management of U.S. military bases in Japan, the U.S. nuclear umbrella, and the role of the Japanese military beyond the mission of self-defense. The U.S. military bases in Japan had long drawn criticism; as such, the DPJ's primary interest in its early formulation of alliance-management goals seemed to be the SOFA and the realignment of U.S. bases.

## JAPAN'S BASING POLICIES

The U.S. and Japanese governments agreed to realign U.S. forces in Japan in 2006, including closing U.S. Marine Air Station Futenma in Okinawa.[23] The Taro Aso cabinet concluded the implementation agreement for moving U.S. Marines to Guam and constructing a new runway in northern Okinawa in February 2009, and consultations on the consolidation plan began with the governor of Okinawa, Hirokazu Nakaima.[24] His response to the proposal was due to be discussed with the national government in October. In his meeting with Prime Minister Hatoyama, just weeks after the DPJ came into office, the governor was told that the new government was taking another look at the relocation plan.

The political coalition of the DPJ, JSP, and the People's New Party came into office arguing for a reduced number of U.S. forces in Okinawa and a review of the base consolidation plan put forward by their predecessors. Yukio Hatoyama had campaigned in Okinawa just weeks before the lower house election, and had promised that his party would relocate U.S. Marine Air Station Futenma to another prefecture. His coalition partners, especially the JSP, had long opposed the relocation of Air Station Futenma on Okinawa, and indeed had argued that the U.S. Marines should relocate to the U.S. mainland rather than somewhere else in Japan. By the end of 2009, the prime minister put together a new task force comprising his coalition partners to consider different options for Futenma. Even Secretary-General Ozawa traveled to Naha to reassure DPJ supporters.

Other members of the cabinet were also responsible for policymaking on Okinawa. Japan's new defense minister, Toshimi Kitazawa, made an early visit to Okinawa to meet with the governor and mayors of both Ginowan City, home to the U.S. Marine Air Station Futenma, and Nago City, the prospective site for the relocation.[25] Foreign Minister Katsuya Okada began discussions with the U.S. ambassador to Japan, John Roos, on the decision-making to date on the Futenma relocation. The minister for land, infrastructure, transport, and tourism, Seiji Maehara, also visited the island to consult with the prefectural government and others on the existing relocation plan. After reviewing the plans previously considered as alternatives to Nago City as the site for the U.S. Marine helicopters, Prime Minister Hatoyama put forward his own relocation proposal despite objections from some in his cabinet. In early April 2010, the Japanese media reported Hatoyama was considering the construction of an alternative facility on Tokunoshima, an island that is part of Kyushu Prefecture and 200 kilometers (124 miles) north of the main island of Okinawa.[26] The proposal called for construction of a runway that would allow as many as 2,500 U.S. Marines to move to the island. By the end of the month, however, local sentiment in Tokunoshima was strongly against the Hatoyama plan, and even those who were thought to have originally signaled their receptivity were publicly opposed.[27]

The DPJ also targeted the SOFA for reform. In particular, local governments in regions with U.S. forces were concerned about their ability to manage environmental oversight of the bases. The Japan Governors Association, which represented the fourteen prefectures that host U.S. bases and was co-chaired by the governors of Kanagawa and Okinawa Prefectures, proposed an environmental agreement that would attach to the SOFA, and visited Washington, DC, to discuss its ideas for SOFA revision.[28] The Obama administration worked on the details of the proposal, and in December 2013, as Governor Nakaima at long last approved the relocation plan for Futenma, the United States and Japan announced the launch of bilateral consultations toward producing an environmental management agreement on U.S. forces in Japan.[29] Rather than the DPJ, it was the LDP's Abe cabinet that finalized the deal with Okinawa's governor.

## NUCLEAR WEAPONS

The DPJ also took aim at one of the long-standing policies of the LDP regarding the potential use of nuclear weapons. Former officials had openly discussed the existence of secret agreements between the LDP government and the United States to employ nuclear weapons on Japan's behalf. When the DPJ came into office, Foreign Minister Katsuya Okada ordered an internal investigation in the Ministry of Foreign Affairs (MOFA) of these agreements and organized an expert oversight committee to examine MOFA's archives.[30]

Though the findings were inconclusive on the ultimate question of Japanese government acquiescence to the use of nuclear weapons on Japan's behalf, the move cleared the air for a discussion in the Japanese parliament on whether it would be beneficial for Japan to allow use of the weapons in the case of a conflict. In parliament, Foreign Minister Okada argued that Japan's experience with nuclear weapons continued to inform his government's position on their use, but he pointed out that in the event of a conflict, future leaders would have to decide whether allowing the United States to introduce nuclear weapons into a conflict would be in Japan's best interests at the time.[31] Transparency about past practices thus cleared the way for the first honest discussion in the Diet about Japan's ultimate reliance on the U.S. nuclear deterrent. Japan and the United States initiated extended deterrence consultations afterward that allowed Japan to shape the Obama administration's thinking on its Nuclear Posture Review (NPR).[32]

The DPJ went on to become a partner with the United States and others in United Nations (UN) nonproliferation cooperation efforts on North Korea.[33] As foreign minister and deputy prime minister in the Yoshihiko Noda cabinet, Okada also presided over Japan's deliberations regarding cooperation on nonproliferation sanctions against Iran. After an extended examination of Japan's interests in its long-standing relationship with Iran, Okada designed a Japanese approach to supporting the nonproliferation sanctions devised by the United States and the other Permanent Five, or P5, countries (Russia, China, United Kingdom, and France).[34] In December 2011, Japan announced restrictions on 106 entities with links to proliferation-sensitive activities in Iran. The following March, Tokyo took additional steps to terminate banking relationships and freeze Iranian assets in Japan.[35]

## THE ROLE OF THE SELF-DEFENSE FORCE

Finally, the DPJ was cautious about changing the interpretation of Japan's constitution or weakening civilian control over the military. Of course, by then Japan had decided to send its Self-Defense Force (SDF) overseas to join UN Peacekeeping Operations (PKO), and an UN-centric notion of collective security had gained some support among both conservative and liberal legislators.[36] The Japanese public grew more accustomed to their military's participation in peacekeeping operations. The SDF has participated in thirteen PKO missions to date, including in Cambodia, East Timor, Haiti, and most recently South Sudan.[37] Even before winning election, the DPJ had endorsed SDF participation "under national control and democratic oversight" in UN operations that would contribute to maintaining peace. The deployments of 2,200 SDF personnel for humanitarian relief operations in Haiti and another 400 to peacekeeping operations in South Sudan were made by DPJ governments.[38]

Yet before they came into office, the DPJ wanted to ensure limits on the use of the SDF in coalition military operations, in particular, in U.S.-led coalition efforts in Iraq. The Koizumi cabinet had already pledged Japanese support for the United States in the wake of the 9/11 attacks. As an opposition party, the DPJ had been a thorn in the side of the Koizumi cabinet as it sought to assist the Bush administration in Operation Enduring Freedom in Iraq. U.S. requests for coalition assistance in refueling operations led Japan to consider using the Maritime Self-Defense Force (MSDF), and ultimately Japan refueled almost a thousand ships in the Indian Ocean—operating primarily near Oman and Yemen, including Oman Bay and the Gulf of Aden—despite considerable opposition in the Diet from the DPJ.[39]

Even as the DPJ sought to limit Japan's involvement in the Iraq War, some legislators saw opportunity to advocate for a SDF role in antipiracy operations in the Gulf of Aden.[40] In October 2008, after extended discussions on Japan's support for U.S.-led military operations in Iraq, DPJ member Akihisa Nagashima argued that the Japanese government should look ahead to the upcoming transition in the U.S. government, noting then presidential candidate Barack Obama's emphasis on shifting U.S. counterterrorism focus from Iraq to Afghanistan. However, Nagashima's real aim was to propose that Japan take on antipiracy efforts in the Gulf of Aden, a mission that he argued would be consistent with Japanese interests but also could be seen as a contribution to coalition efforts to stabilize sea lanes. Prime Minister Taro Aso reacted with surprise, saying that it sounded more like an LDP idea than a DPJ idea.[41] But the initiative was viewed positively within the LDP government and also gained traction within the DPJ as a way for the SDF to play a constructive coalition role in sea-lane defenses for Middle Eastern trade routes.[42]

Two other policy areas also influenced the U.S.-Japan alliance in recent years. The first was the DPJ's management of Japan's regular defense planning process. New National Defense Program Guidelines (NDPG) were due for approval by the end of 2009, just months after the DPJ came into office. Instead of approving the draft crafted under the Aso cabinet, the Hatoyama cabinet postponed discussion

for a year. A new advisory committee was established and its recommendations were presented to the Naoto Kan cabinet in August
2010.[43] At its core, the new NDPG argued for a "dynamic defense posture," abandoning the basic defense posture that had guided Japanese
defense planning since the 1970s.[44] The Ministry of Defense aimed to
build a military force with improved readiness, organized to respond
flexibly to new contingencies.[45]

Defense spending also came under scrutiny. The DPJ initiated a
review of government spending as part of its campaign promise to rid
the Japanese budget of waste.[46] All bureaucracies were instructed to cut
their annual budgets, and the Ministry of Defense was expected to con-
form. In the end, Defense Minister Kitazawa argued for some latitude
for his ministry, but Japan's defense spending declined to its lowest levels
in more than a decade during the DPJ years. In absolute terms, Japan's
defense budget declined annually by 0.4 percent during the DPJ's time
in office.[47] Despite this pressure on Japan's military spending, the DPJ
government approved a new five-year agreement with Washington to
maintain host nation support for U.S. forces in Japan at the fiscal year
(FY) 2010 level of 188.1 billion yen ($2.02 billion).[48]

But perhaps the most important influence on DPJ thinking about
greater military cooperation between the SDF and U.S. military came
as a result of the disastrous Great East Japan Earthquake of 2011. In
Operation Tomodachi, the United States mobilized support for the
SDF's relief effort.[49] The U.S. military, at its peak, had approximately
24,000 personnel, 189 aircraft, and 24 navy vessels involved in the
humanitarian assistance and relief efforts.[50] The SDF operated from
U.S. ships near the areas hardest hit by the earthquake and tsunami, and
the U.S. military followed the SDF's lead in organizing recovery efforts.
U.S. Marines reopened Sendai airport, which was devastated by the
tsunami, allowing relief forces and supplies to be flown in to the Tohoku
region. Years of training undertaken by the SDF and U.S. forces facilitated cooperation. However, the two militaries had few plans for one of
their most important missions: managing the meltdowns of reactors at
the Fukushima Daiichi nuclear plant.[51] A task force led jointly by Goshi
Hosono of the Japanese government and Ambassador John Roos at the
U.S. embassy coordinated the alliance's response to the nuclear crisis.
The DPJ government relied heavily on the United States as it sought to
respond to Japan's largest disaster since World War II.

## JAPAN'S REGIONAL RELATIONS

The DPJ further distinguished itself through its approach to Japan's neighbors. Although Hatoyama's early advocacy for an "East Asian community" suggested that the DPJ would emphasize its relations with China and South Korea over those with the United States, this was not the policy agenda that emerged once the DPJ came into power. Many of the conclusions drawn about the DPJ's idea of an East Asian community were premature. Indeed, there seemed to be little development of the concept. At the September 2009 meeting of the UN General Assembly, Hatoyama briefly mentioned the East Asian community in his speech but did not go into much detail.[52] At the Asia-Pacific Economic Cooperation (APEC) summit meeting that November, Hatoyama expanded on his idea of an East Asian community, but this time emphasized the importance of the U.S. presence in Asia.[53]

Rather than a strategic reorientation away from Washington, the DPJ's emphasis on Japan's relations with its Northeast Asian neighbors came from its long-held commitment to postwar reconciliation. Japan's liberals had long advocated for acknowledging their country's wartime behavior and directly addressing the consequences for postwar Japanese. Political realignment in Japan changed the way the Japanese government approached reconciliation with China and South Korea, but it did not erase differences between liberals and conservatives over their positions on Japan's twentieth-century history.

The two major statements of Japanese remorse for the past—the 1993 Kono Statement, issued on the system of wartime military brothels organized for use by the Imperial Army, and the 1995 Murayama Statement, issued on Japan's imperial conquest—coincided with the end of LDP dominance. The Kono Statement was developed under an LDP prime minister, Kiichi Miyazawa, and named for his chief cabinet secretary, Yohei Kono.[54] But it was issued shortly after the July 1993 general election brought the first liberal coalition to power to form the Hosokawa cabinet. More notable for its substantive impact on policy, the coalition that followed of the LDP and the JSP, odd bedfellows and longtime nemeses during the Cold War, resulted in the 1995 Murayama Statement on Japan's past, an unhesitant statement of Japanese responsibility and remorse for the suffering caused by its imperial aggression in the earlier half of the twentieth century.[55]

When it came into office more than a decade later, the DPJ heartily concurred with the Murayama Statement and worked closely with MOFA and its counterparts in South Korea to craft Japan's statement of remorse on the one hundredth anniversary of Japan's colonization of the Korean peninsula.[56]

The DPJ, however, took an ambiguous stance on another issue of reconciliation: the politically sensitive Kono Statement. In August 2012, DPJ prime minister Yoshihiko Noda reaffirmed the Japanese government's commitment to the Kono Statement, speaking before the upper house budget committee, but repeated what many in the LDP had often stated: there was no direct evidence that the so-called comfort women were forced into servicing Japanese troops by the Imperial Army.[57] When it came to the question of compensation for those who had borne the brunt of Japanese colonial history, the DPJ was more comfortable addressing those who had served as prisoners of war, and hesitated to articulate a clear approach to the victims of sexual slavery.

Japan's relations with Seoul had a direct impact on its relations with Washington. Trilateral cooperation with South Korea and the United States on North Korea had been forged in the wake of the 1998 firing of a Taepodong missile over Japan, and the U.S. effort to manage nuclear proliferation by Pyongyang had centered on alliance cooperation with South Korea and Japan. In 2012, Japan's relations with South Korea took a worrisome turn, however, when President Lee Myung-bak visited the disputed islands of Takeshima/Dokdo and openly chastised Japan over its lack of sufficient remorse for its history. Lee's actions coincided with growing tensions between China and Japan over their territorial dispute, and led to the worst diplomatic estrangement between Tokyo and Seoul since the conclusion of their peace treaty in 1965. Diplomatic tensions over the legacies of Japan's twentieth-century imperial expansion in Asia were not directly linked to Japan's alliance cooperation with Washington, but were increasingly shaping the ability of the United States to rely on its two Northeast Asian allies to manage the growing security risk from North Korea. Despite the DPJ's emphasis on careful management of Japan's ties with South Korea, the diplomatic relationship was frayed by the time the party left office, as domestic politics in Tokyo and Seoul ushered in a new phase of contention over their differences over the past.

# The LDP's Alliance Reform Agenda

The LDP returned to power in 2012 a different party. Of the LDP's members elected in 2012 and 2013, 119 from the lower house and 37 from the upper house were first-time legislators. Thus, of the 408 total LDP Diet members, roughly one-third were new to governance. Moreover, the LDP was faced with a notably different parliament. The DPJ was significantly weaker, but the new *Nippon Ishin no Kai* (Japan Restoration Party), a conservative, antiestablishment party, presented an ideologically divided opposition. Internally, however, the LDP could no longer rely on its own structures of policy analysis and advocacy, structures that for much of its postwar history were impervious to external influences. Secretary-General Shigeru Ishiba understood better than anyone that the LDP had to increase its transparency and accountability to the Japanese voter. Having been banished to the opposition once, the LDP could not afford to rest on its laurels, despite its electoral success in both houses of parliament.

Moreover, territorial disputes emerged at the forefront of Japan's relations with its neighbors. The 2010 collision of a Chinese fishing trawler and two Japanese Coast Guard ships led to criticism of the DPJ for not standing up to Chinese pressure and prompted considerable domestic advocacy for stronger Japanese defense of the disputed islands. Tokyo governor Shintaro Ishihara openly challenged the Noda cabinet by offering to buy the islands to ensure that they remained out of Chinese hands.[58] The Abe cabinet came into office amid rising tensions between Beijing and Tokyo over the Senkaku/Diaoyu Islands. In the leadership contest for the LDP in September 2012, four of the five candidates spoke to Japan's strong conviction to protect its sovereignty. Shinzo Abe argued that the government should station officials on the islands to ensure effective control.

Though Japan's tensions with China over the islands have dominated the headlines since 2012, Japan's relations with South Korea have also been strained. The linkage between territorial sovereignty disputes and pent-up frustration over the postwar settlement in Northeast Asia has made the restoration of security cooperation between Seoul and Tokyo increasingly difficult. Trilateral U.S.-Japan-South Korea cooperation on North Korea, for example, though still ongoing, has lost much of its momentum. Likewise, opportunities for greater bilateral security cooperation have stalled.

Abe's party, like the new conservative *Ishin no Kai*, campaigned on "restoring" Japan, returning it to its former strength. The focal point of the LDP's reform agenda was economic policy and a new program, dubbed Abenomics, sought to use fiscal, monetary, and structural innovation to stimulate growth. This theme of restoring Japan also fed into Abe's security policy agenda. In February 2013, Abe declared that "Japan is back" at a speech in Washington, DC, signaling his intention to pursue a more proactive and visible role in the alliance and in global affairs.[59] Abe's agenda included significant reforms in Japan's security planning, but Abe also raised concerns about his approach to Japan's national statements on history.

## DEFENSE REFORM

The Abe cabinet's defense reforms began immediately. His defense minister, Itsunori Onodera, announced that he would revise the National Defense Program Guidelines drafted just a year earlier under the DPJ. Moreover, the prime minister announced that Japan would establish a National Security Council (NSC), a reform he had proposed during his first term in 2006. Accompanying the NSC was a secrecy protection law, long a priority of U.S. governments as a prerequisite to closer military cooperation. By the end of 2013, the Abe cabinet had passed legislation in the Diet for both the NSC and the secrecy law, and in a December cabinet resolution Abe announced a new National Security Strategy and a revised NDPG accompanied by an updated five-year defense plan.[60]

The alliance was also on the agenda for an upgrade. In the final months of the DPJ's Noda cabinet, Defense Minister Satoshi Morimoto had proposed a review of the bilateral defense cooperation guidelines, and the following year, under the Abe cabinet, the U.S. secretaries of state and defense met in Tokyo with the new foreign and defense ministers to announce that these guidelines would be revised by December 2014.[61]

This would be the second revision of the U.S.-Japan military division of labor. Seventeen years earlier, the guidelines were revamped for a post–Cold War Asia, paving the way for a review of Japan's defense planning legislation.[62] The 2014 guidelines are expected to accompany a reinterpretation of Japan's constitution to allow the SDF to use force on behalf of the United States and other regional security partners.[63]

The Abe cabinet's relaxation of restrictions on the export of arms was also significant, albeit less debated. A new policy governing the transfer of defense-related technology was adopted on April 1, 2014, and sets forth the principles guiding Japan's defense industry's cooperation with other powers.[64] Talks are already under way with Australia, India, and several Southeast Asian states on the use of Japanese defense technologies.[65]

## CRISIS MANAGEMENT AND THE SENKAKU/DIAOYU ISLANDS

Beyond the initial statements made by Prime Minister Abe on how to ensure Japan's sovereignty over the Senkaku/Diaoyu Islands, the Abe cabinet has sought to maintain calm and seek diplomatic talks with Beijing. In and around the islands' waters, the LDP has continued policies introduced by the Noda cabinet. New ships have been procured for the Japanese coast guard and the government is reviewing the overall management of gray zone situations below the level of armed force. These scenarios, including disputes over the islands, are included in the broader defense reform discussions and the U.S.-Japan Defense Cooperation Guidelines.

The Chinese announcement of an Air Defense Identification Zone (ADIZ) in November 2013 raised the prospect of a more militarized interaction between Chinese and Japanese forces in the East China Sea.[66] The Abe cabinet has refused to acknowledge the Chinese ADIZ, both for its military operations as well as for civilian airliners. Rules of engagement for the Air Self-Defense Force (ASDF) were confirmed in January 2013, and surveillance of the East China Sea was upgraded. The ASDF scrambled against Chinese aircraft 415 times in FY2013 (up from 306 times in FY2012), and the Japanese government has protested recent close-proximity interactions between its surveillance aircraft and armed Chinese fighter jets in the East China Sea.[67]

The Abe cabinet has also sought continued reassurance from Washington on its security commitment to the Senkaku/Diaoyu Islands. On his visit to Tokyo in April 2014, President Obama repeated the long-standing U.S. position that the U.S.-Japan security treaty covers the islands, which are under Japan's administrative control.[68] Earlier that month, U.S. defense secretary Chuck Hagel traveled to both Tokyo and Beijing, emphasizing the alliance commitment to respond to coercion.[69] The Obama administration had also begun to challenge Chinese claims in the South China Sea as Beijing sought to assert its rights unilaterally regarding its Southeast Asian neighbors.[70]

## JAPAN'S REGIONAL RELATIONS

Abe came into the prime minister's office in December 2012 as tensions with China were on the rise over the Senkaku/Diaoyu Islands and after President Lee Myung-bak's visit to the islets of Dokdo/Takeshima highlighted Japan's territorial dispute with South Korea. A new South Korean president was elected just days after Abe's LDP won a majority in Japan's lower house, and President Park Geun-hye premised her vision of Northeast Asia community building on a "correct understanding of history."[71] Japan's regional relations were deteriorating rapidly, and neither Beijing nor Seoul proved enthusiastic about turning their bilateral relations with Tokyo around.

Although Abe did not create these tensions, his cabinet raised new questions about Japan's ability to navigate the difficult diplomacy emerging in Northeast Asia. Early in his term, media reports that Abe was thinking of abandoning the 1993 Kono and 1995 Murayama Statements—seen as evidence of Japan's desire for reconciliation with China and South Korea—were ultimately denied by Chief Cabinet Secretary Yoshihide Suga.[72] Yet the prime minister's interest in crafting a new statement, one that did not rely on the legacy of Japan's expansion and war on the Asian continent, fostered concerns abroad that the carefully crafted national policy on regional reconciliation would be revised.[73] Domestic sentiments in Japan were also a source of political pressure. The politicization of Japan's territorial dispute with South Korea, in addition to its island disputes with China, produced a large downturn in popular sentiment.[74]

The reemergence of tensions over historical memory also made the improvement in diplomacy with China and South Korea difficult. The sensitive question of a Japanese apology to the women forcibly recruited for military brothels gained new political momentum in 2011, when the Korean supreme court called for reopening diplomatic discussions over the Korean victims. President Lee raised the issue with Abe's predecessor, Yoshihiko Noda, during their summit meeting in 2012, and the Ministry of Foreign Affairs tried and failed to find a diplomatic compromise. The election of a new South Korean president offered an opportunity, but the Abe cabinet had little success in its outreach to President Park. Abe's past statements on the issue of sexual slavery denied that there was evidence of direct responsibility by the Imperial Army, and the Diet demand for an investigation of the Kono Statement raised fears that Abe would rescind Japan's statement of remorse to the women victimized during World War II.[75]

On March 14, 2014, after months of speculation about the Abe cabinet's intentions regarding the Kono Statement, Abe clearly stated that he would maintain it as national policy, but agreed to an expert review of the evidence in question.[76] The results of the policy review, announced on June 20, spoke to domestic critics of the Kono Statement, refuting their contention that it was based on too much compromise with the South Korean government and too little evidence in support of the women's testimonials.[77] Like the effort of the DPJ to review the internal policy deliberations over the government's position on the use of nuclear weapons by the United States to defend Japan, the Abe cabinet sought to dispel suspicions of collusion with foreign governments over Japan's policy choices and provide greater accountability on the choice of issuing a statement of remorse for the system of military brothels. Suspicions of Japan's foreign policy decision-making now emanate from both ends of the political spectrum.

Similarly, the Abe cabinet has had little success in its efforts to open a direct dialogue with China's new leader, Xi Jinping. In January 2013, Natsuo Yamaguchi, president of Komeito, the LDP's coalition partner, visited China and met with Xi, raising hopes for a diplomatic opening. Masahiko Komura, vice president of the LDP and chair of the bipartisan Japan-China Parliamentary Friendship Association, along with the DPJ's Katsuya Okada, planned to visit Beijing, but the group canceled the trip in April 2013 when it became clear that the delegates would be unable to meet with Xi. The Chinese announcement of an ADIZ in the East China Sea in November soured relations further. Komura's delegation, including Okada, finally visited Beijing in May 2014 and held talks with Zhang Dejiang, the third-ranking member of the Chinese Politburo Standing Committee. In the talks, Komura conveyed Prime Minister Abe's desire for a summit meeting with President Xi in the near future.

Japan's difficult diplomacy with South Korea and China had a direct impact on the alliance. Of particular concern was the protracted estrangement between Tokyo and Seoul. High-level efforts by the Obama administration to reduce tensions between Tokyo and Seoul were initially unsuccessful. U.S. vice president Joseph R. Biden Jr. seemed unable to broker a compromise when he visited both capitals in November 2013, and when Prime Minister Abe visited the controversial Yasukuni Shrine on December 26, he drew intense criticism from South Korea and an expression of "disappointment" from the United States.[78] A direct intervention by the White House facilitated a trilateral summit meeting in March 2014 at The Hague with President Obama, Prime Minister Abe, and President Park to discuss their common security concerns over North Korea and helped create the opportunity for direct talks between the Japanese and South Korean governments on war legacy issues.[79] Regarding China, U.S. officials repeatedly visited both Tokyo and Beijing to advocate for a reduction in tensions in the East China Sea. Secretary of Defense Hagel's trip to Beijing and Tokyo and President Obama's visit to Tokyo in April 2014 clearly outlined the U.S. defense commitment to Japan. In both cases, the aim was twofold: to ensure no miscalculation by China over U.S. interests in the event of a confrontation and to reassure Japan that the United States would be there to help should China opt to use force.

The delicate politics of alliance management continue to be shaped by Japan's domestic politics, even since the conservatives' return to power in 2012. The issues that shape the alliance dialogue remain constant over time, but the emphases of Japan's liberals and conservatives differ. The complex diplomatic relations in Northeast Asia—once seen as separate from alliance concerns—now overlap in conspicuous ways, as Seoul and Beijing increasingly contest Japan's positions on historical memory and its security provisions with Washington. The island dispute between Japan and China has also changed the alliance security balance, and the United States today must imagine the possibility that, for the first time in the postwar period, Japan may be the target of aggression and that the United States will need to organize itself to assist Japan against a rising China.

# Reforming Japan's Policymaking

Japan's debate over political reform since the mid-1990s has focused on changing the way policy is made. Though broad differences over the constitution and Japan's prewar past shaped conservative and liberal foreign policy choices, the political debate that emerged—particularly after Prime Minister Koizumi's tenure—was largely about the process of policymaking.[80] The ambitions of Japan's conservatives and liberals have coincided on several aspects of policy reform.

First, politicians of all stripes sought to elevate their policymaking roles, thereby rebalancing the part played by Japan's bureaucrats. This idea found support across the political spectrum, especially regarding domestic policymaking. For example, Koizumi advocated for small government and the privatization of the postal services in his campaign for the 2005 lower house, specifically asking whether the Japanese people wanted so many bureaucrats determining their future.[81]

A more "inside Kasumigaseki" incident in the Koizumi era highlighted the growing tension between Japan's much-vaunted civil servants and its leading politicians over who had control over policymaking. In April 2001, Koizumi appointed Makiko Tanaka, the daughter of former LDP prime minister Kakuei Tanaka, as foreign minister, largely because of her electoral popularity. Yet within months, Tanaka was locked into a struggle with the MOFA bureaucrats. Media reports of Minister Tanaka barricading herself in the ministry's personnel division in an attempt to override the regular personnel process created tremendous drama for the rather staid Japanese ministry, and ultimately the showdown resulted in Koizumi asking Tanaka to step down and the senior vice foreign minister to retire.[82]

The DPJ was also at loggerheads with Japan's bureaucrats. The early years of the DPJ tenure were replete with media stories about politicians unwilling to share decision-making with the bureaucrats and skeptical of their loyalty.[83] The DPJ took aim at two practices that revealed the institutionalized preferences given to Japan's civil servants. It sought to end the practice of *amakudari* (descending from heaven), wherein bureaucrats received high-profile posts in the private sector upon retiring from their ministry. Bringing in experts from outside the bureaucracy was seen as a way to open Japan's policymaking process to allow experts from outside to have a greater voice.

The DPJ also sought to amplify the role of politicians in the policymaking process by downgrading the regular administrative processes run by the bureaucrats. In the first DPJ cabinet, some cabinet ministers excluded bureaucrats from meetings whereas others supported a more consultative relationship. The DPJ hurt its governance capacity, however, by ending the regular administrative vice ministers' meeting that coordinated policy across ministries. Prime Minister Yoshihiko Noda reinstated these meetings in the third DPJ cabinet. In the end, both the LDP and DPJ would have to curb their ambitions and mend fences with Japan's bureaucrats.

Second, Japan's politicians sought to centralize policymaking to create institutions capable of crafting national strategy and integrating policy implementation. In 2009, the DPJ created a National Strategy Office—loosely based on the British effort to develop an advisory body to the prime minister—led by the deputy prime minister, Naoto Kan. This body comprised politicians and was responsible for formulating Japan's national strategy. Ultimately, a new National Strategy Bureau was to be designed that would coordinate economic, foreign, and national security policy, but this did not materialize.[84] The LDP had long debated the formation of a U.S.-style NSC, and the Abe cabinet successfully passed legislation to create its own in December 2013. Shortly thereafter, a National Security Strategy was issued.

Finally, from Koizumi's populism to Kan's citizen activism, Japan's political leaders were increasingly interested in appealing to the Japanese public for support in reforming Japan. Koizumi was tagged as a populist because he threw down the gauntlet to those in his party who resisted privatization reform, calling a general election to explore the public's preferences. Kan, in contrast, began his political career as a grassroots activist and ultimately took on Japan's bureaucrats in the Ministry of Health, Labor, and Welfare when he found that they had sided with Japanese pharmaceutical companies to prevent access to

drugs for HIV/AIDS patients. Politicians like Koizumi and Kan campaigned on the premise that Japan's citizens needed better representation in policy decisions. But their political success also depended on the
growing popular demand for better governance.

The transfer of power in Japan in 2009 to a new party revealed, however, that the institutional supports for this new type of politics were inad-
equate. Japan's policymaking process had been designed over decades of
single-party dominance, and the defining role of the LDP and its internal
debates over policy had concentrated policy analysis and priority setting
within the party. The lack of transparency about how policy choices had
been analyzed in the past as well as the lack of institutional memory on
past decisions clearly hampered the DPJ government when it came into
office. There were simply no standards by which to measure past policymaking outside narrow parochial politics. Moreover, the weakness of
the parliamentary committees as a venue for policy deliberation was also
clear. The Diet committees were largely seen as forums of contention and
there was little desire to bring committee members into a more constructive—and cross-party—dialogue on policy priorities and preferences.

Reshaping Japan's policymaking on the U.S.-Japan alliance was a
DPJ priority. Although the DPJ's impact on the alliance is evidence of
Japan's new reform politics, it is often overstated or misunderstood.
First, though much has been made of the alliance difficulties during
the DPJ's time in office, the party did not advocate a dramatic change
in alliance policy goals. Even the contentious Futenma relocation effort
was more about how best to respond to the grievances of the people
of Okinawa than about serious differences over the need for U.S. military forces in Japan. The DPJ never asked the United States to remove
the Marines from Japan, nor did it refute the need for an alternative air
base for them. Rather, the Hatoyama cabinet found itself unprepared
to implement an alternative to relocation within the Okinawa Prefecture, and within months, abandoned its plan to find an alternative site,
thereby undermining its support in Okinawa.[85] Inexperience and an
inability to implement a change in policy led to Hatoyama's resignation,
and though his downfall was largely a result of pressures from within
his ruling coalition, the DPJ's early focus on the Okinawa base plan
poisoned his relationship with Washington.[86] Even the DPJ's powerful
secretary-general, Ichiro Ozawa, seemed unable to navigate the complex pressures of base politics in Okinawa.

Second, partisanship, rather than policy differences, often prevented cooperation between the DPJ and LDP. The DPJ brought into the government a new generation of politicians with little or no experience in security and foreign policy, but the LDP often portrayed them as ideologically driven. Much of the criticism of the party highlighted the ideological differences between the LDP and the DPJ, but these differences were far less pronounced once the DPJ took office. Yet while the DPJ governed, the LDP was loath to find common cause, even on policies it had once authored and continued to support. The DPJ received little LDP support in its effort to review the Okinawa basing agreement or to manage a more contentious relationship with Beijing. Even on policies related to disaster relief, the LDP found it difficult to offer support to the DPJ government in implementing crisis response. Cross-party cooperation on alliance issues has been slow to emerge in Japan, and though today the DPJ's criticisms of Prime Minister Abe's security agenda may be more muted than in the past, the party remains divided over military cooperation between Japan and the United States.

Third, change in the agenda of alliance cooperation was more often than not prompted by external events than by party preferences. Naoto Kan's tenure was shaped by two crises that strengthened cooperation between the new DPJ government and Washington: a run-in with China over a fishing trawler in waters near the Senkaku/Diaoyu Islands and the Great East Japan Earthquake and tsunami. A new phase of alliance cooperation in the recovery process, Operation Tomodachi, focused bilateral attention on crisis response, including the effort to cope with the meltdown at the Fukushima Daiichi nuclear power plant. Japan's triple disasters changed the DPJ's relationship with the United States, but the DPJ, even by its third prime minister, Yoshihiko Noda, continued to be confronted by Japan's conservatives over its handling of foreign policy as tensions with China reemerged over the disputed islands. By the time the LDP returned to power in December 2012, with Shinzo Abe as its leader and Japan's prime minister, the Obama administration and the new DPJ government had resolved their early differences, but Japan's diplomatic relations with its neighbors had deteriorated.

Neither party found it easy to manage externally generated crises or demand for policy adaptation. The 2010 crisis with Beijing over the Chinese fishing trawler in Senkaku/Diaoyu waters confounded both parties. Parliamentary debate in the aftermath of the two-week tensions focused on the DPJ's inadequacies, but the LDP leaders who had strong ties with Beijing also were hard pressed to find avenues for dialogue. Moreover, as the LDP and DPJ quibbled in the Diet over the DPJ's management of the crisis, policymakers in Washington and in other regional capitals were quick to focus instead on the Chinese confrontational response, including the imposition of an informal embargo of rare earth materials exports to Japan and the arrest of Japanese businessmen in China.[87]

Abe's alliance reform agenda also faces challenges. The territorial dispute with China and a severely strained political standoff with South Korea have created some tricky politics for the Japanese government, both at home and abroad. Partisanship has seeped into Japan's foreign policy debate in new ways. Even as the Abe cabinet argues that the LDP is the true steward of the U.S.-Japan alliance, undercurrents of strain between Tokyo and Washington over Abe's visit to the controversial Yasukuni Shrine suggest that the Abe government may be hard-pressed to gain unequivocal support from Washington.

Fourth, much has been made of the discomfort of Japan's political transition for alliance managers in both countries, but there is a danger in overstating the DPJ's legacy. Leadership transitions in democracies are often time-consuming and at times contentious processes. In Washington, too, alternating parties in power often cause disconnects in U.S. foreign policymaking.[88] The two major transitions in Japan's government in 2009 and in 2012 were managed, however, by a single U.S. administration—that of Obama. Alliance management could have been further complicated had the United States also changed parties in the midst of DPJ rule in Japan.

A larger and perhaps less examined premise about the impact of Japanese domestic politics and the U.S.-Japan alliance is that single-party dominance in Japan produced a predictable framework for managing the security cooperation between Tokyo and Washington. For the most part, U.S. policymakers rely heavily on Japan's bureaucrats for the day-to-day management of the relationship. Nonetheless, political change even within the LDP has often prompted policy change. Today, with a new generation coming to the fore in Japanese politics, and with more parties now contending for coalition government in Japan, U.S. policymakers will need to work harder to keep pace with the emerging policymaking context in Tokyo.

# Implications for Alliance Management

Democratic governments regularly change parties in power, and for Washington policymakers, the changing of the guard in their alliance partners rarely signals a challenge to the foundation of the relationship. In Europe, U.S. allies in Great Britain, Germany, and other countries in the North Atlantic Treaty Organization (NATO) have often elected governments that were critical of some aspect of alliance cooperation. During the Cold War, politics within allied states often centered on issues that involved U.S. policy choices or demands for alliance cooperation by governments that sat uncomfortably with their publics. In Asia, too, allies of the United States often amended or changed their policies based on domestic leadership changes. Australia regularly moved from conservative to labor party dominance in the parliament. South Korea's presidential system created an even more complex balancing act for alliance policy as the process of democratization pitted pro-alliance leaders against those who sought greater autonomy from the United States. Reorganizing U.S. forces in South Korea and the transfer of wartime operational control were negotiated as a result of political transitions in Seoul. Democratization in the Philippines also brought some fundamental changes to U.S. military strategy in the region when a post–Ferdinand Marcos senate decided not to renew the bilateral basing agreement.[89]

Single-party dominance in Japan since 1955 did not protect the alliance from domestic contention. Despite its electoral majority, the LDP was confronted regularly in parliament over its management of alliance relations with the United States. Focal points of contention remained remarkably consistent over time, and included questions related to the SDF and its role in military cooperation with U.S. forces, the role of nuclear weapons by the United States and their storage in Japan, and the management of U.S. bases in Japan. Thus, when the LDP weakened in the early 1990s and new parties were being formed, these issues

continued to inform debate over the implementation of security cooperation between the United States and Japan.

As political reform in Japan progressed, it was clear that the United
States was beginning to ask more of the alliance. From the Gulf War
to the response to 9/11, coalition military responses in the Middle East
were increasingly the norm. Asia too had its own transformations that
changed the region's security relationships. North Korea's nuclear and
missile proliferation, repeated disaster and humanitarian crises, and the
growing economic and military reach of China prompted new consider-
ations as to how the United States and Japan could adjust their strategic
cooperation. Japan's political reforms coincided with this geostrategic
shift, and many see a direct causal relationship. Whether correlation
or causation, however, the LDP lost its ability to dominate politics pre-
cisely when Washington was looking to Tokyo to make unprecedented
decisions about its military's role in supporting contingency planning
and broader cooperation with other U.S. allies in regional security.

Japan's protracted process of political change, therefore, came at
a time of growing U.S. expectations of the alliance. For many in the
United States, the seemingly unending process of political realignment in Tokyo created uncertainty and no small measure of frustration.
Leadership turnover was high—annual, in fact—the case since the mid-
1990s, when the LDP began to lose its long-standing grip on power. The
hope of developing a two-party system in Japan whereby policy debate
and contest, led by Japan's politicians rather than by its bureaucrats,
would be the result has long since diminished. Instead, rapid leadership
transition, even when carried out within the same party, has elevated
the importance of the bureaucrats in the day-to-day management of alliance relations. Annual turnovers in prime ministers and their cabinets
have been the norm rather than the exception, but the combination of
frequent turnovers at the cabinet level with a new political party that
was unknown and whose goals were difficult to comprehend seemed a
bar too high for the Obama administration. Finally, coalition governments have become the norm, and have had the effect of limiting the
focus on maintaining the coalition rather than on developing and defining alliance policy goals.

For many policymakers, both in Washington and in Tokyo, nostalgia for the five years of leadership by Junichiro Koizumi (2001–2006)
is considerable. Before Koizumi's stint as prime minister, Japanese
analysts in particular worried about an alliance "adrift," and in the

years since Koizumi resigned in 2006, many American policy experts lamented the continued inner turmoil that kept Japan from playing a major role in the alliance or on the broader global stage.[90] Moreover, the growing tensions in Northeast Asia began to have real consequences for the alliance as Pyongyang's nuclear tests and missile proliferation posed greater concerns and as China's maritime activities began to signal a new era of uneasiness about Beijing's commitment to a "peaceful rise." Perhaps because of the growing pressures on the alliance, nostalgia for the Koizumi era continues today. Both Japan's LDP and DPJ foreign policy thinkers recognized the security challenges that were growing in the region, but no prime minister since has been able to stay in office as long as Koizumi or develop the same rapport with a U.S. president.

Although many in Washington, and indeed in Tokyo, see the return to "normal" predictable governing practices as the most obvious result of the LDP's return to power, the return of Japan's conservatives coincided with increasing tensions in Northeast Asia, particularly with China. Prime Minister Abe's defense reforms, including centralizing decision-making in the new NSC and passing the secrecy protection law, were welcomed in Washington as long-overdue improvements in Japan's security planning. But growing concern over Japan's dispute with China over the Senkaku/Diaoyu Islands and increasingly over the prime minister's perspectives on history suggested a new set of challenges for alliance policy coordination.[91]

In Washington as in Tokyo, many alliance policymakers continue to view Japan's political change narrowly and conflate many of the domestic political challenges to the alliance in recent years as a result of the DPJ's time in office. To be sure, the DPJ's inexperience in governing, especially its lack of familiarity with Japan's foreign and security policy making, did result in unprecedented conundrums for U.S. bureaucrats. Yet the issues that were difficult to resolve between Tokyo and Washington during the DPJ's time in office existed for LDP cabinets as well. The local dissatisfaction with U.S. bases in Okinawa and the desire for limiting SDF involvement in coalition military activities beyond the defense of Japan easily come to mind as issues that require careful consideration of domestic politics. These issues troubled LDP lawmakers before the transfer of power to the DPJ, and they continue to challenge the Abe cabinet today. Tokyo's alliance reform agenda, in other words, is less about the transfer of power than is often thought.

Two other factors must be taken into account. First, the growing willingness of many Japanese, experts and nonexperts alike, to challenge some of the basic assumptions about Japan's postwar policymaking practices has just as much relevance to foreign and security policy making as it does to domestic policy choices. Second, Japan now faces considerably more risk to its security policy choices than in the past, and the rising tensions in Northeast Asia between Japan and its neighbors suggest the need for new options and new thinking about how best to pursue Japan's interests. The DPJ did not have a monopoly on that reform agenda; many conservatives, inside and outside the LDP, share the goal of reforming Japan's security policy choices.

U.S. alliance policymakers had little experience with Japan changing its ruling party. The practices in alliance management, or alliance habits, developed over time reflected this single-party dominance in Japan. The LDP—either alone or in coalition—led the Japanese government for almost all of the half century since the first security treaty was concluded in 1952. That was not to say that the alliance was unchallenged by Japanese political leaders, or that the differences within the LDP leaders over how best to manage alliance relations with Washington did not shape the U.S.-Japan agenda. In the halls of parliament, progressive leftist parties like the JSP and the Japan Communist Party led a sturdy opposition to the alliance. Outside government, citizen activism was just as vibrant in Japan as it was in other allied societies. Antiwar and antinuclear movements shaped government policy just as they did in Europe and elsewhere. The presence of U.S. troops on Japanese soil also was a lightning rod for citizen protest in Japan, particularly in Okinawa, just as it has been in South Korea and other allied nations.

Three challenges will confront U.S. policymakers as they seek to work with Japanese government in the years ahead.

First, partisan divisions within Tokyo remain a hurdle to predictable alliance management. However, none to date challenges the fundamental premises of the alliance. The transfer of power from the LDP to the DPJ and back to the LDP has not produced greater understanding and cooperation between these two parties on issues related to the alliance. Rather, it has produced the familiar impulse to change practices that the previous government adopted. The DPJ sought to change the plan for relocating the U.S. Marine Air Station Futenma but failed to produce a viable alternative. The LDP returned to the relocation plan it had negotiated with Governor Nakaima and gained his agreement to approve the construction of a new runway. Yet the upcoming governor's race in Okinawa in the fall of 2014 continues to worry even the LDP about the plan's implementation. National defense planning also remains relatively consistent. The LDP immediately sought to revamp the National Defense Program Guidelines adopted by the DPJ in 2010, but the new version announced a year later was based largely on the conceptual foundations of the DPJ version. Finally, both the DPJ and the LDP had to cope with the growing tensions in Northeast Asia and devise strategies, diplomatic and military, for coping with the new pressures on Japan. The alliance challenges over the past several years have not simply been a product of political change in Tokyo. But the intensifying partisan squabbling—in the Diet and during government transitions—made alliance management far trickier than it had been in the past.

In hindsight, it is clear that many of the DPJ calls for alliance reforms were driven in large part by the pattern of ruling and opposition party politics during the era of LDP dominance. Parliamentary contention over the alliance had dominated postwar politics, and although the Japanese parliament committee structure allowed for policy consultations, more often than not, core issues related to the SDF, alliance integration, and contingency planning raised concerns about Japan's own civilian control and the limits imposed by Article 9 of the postwar constitution. In anticipation of contest, the LDP sought to limit access to information that would foster opposition, and opposition politicians sought to exploit every opportunity to criticize alliance management practices.

Compromise across parties on security policy was available through the party leaders' meetings, but the lack of access to both the policy analysis and the cost-benefit assessments made by the Japanese government as it made policy decisions meant that the rationale for policy decisions was not obvious. Ironically, the DPJ's time in office allowed for an exploration of issues that had long rankled but also allowed for the formulation of cross-party consensus on alliance policies that had not been possible in the past. The debate over U.S. use of nuclear weapons shifted to a conversation over the continued efficacy of the U.S. nuclear deterrent in coping with Chinese modernization of its strategic forces. And the long-standing concern about the concentration of U.S. military bases on the small island of Okinawa once again raised the question of just how many and what kind of U.S. forces should be forward deployed in post–Cold War Asia.

Second, new challenges for Tokyo in regional relations are complicating alliance choices, and in particular the Senkaku/Diaoyu Islands dispute introduces the new challenge of dissuading military action by Beijing against the islands. The announcement by China of a new ADIZ suggests that the shifting military balance in the region will also challenge Tokyo's defenses. The responsibility for avoiding war and managing crises in the context of this new emerging China is mutual, and revising the U.S.-Japan Defense Cooperation Guidelines must take into account a new scenario for potential conflict involving Japan and the United States. But Washington and Tokyo will also need to reassure Japan's neighbors that it continues to abide by its postwar commitment to peaceful dispute resolution. Tokyo's diplomacy, as well as Washington's, must also focus on building regional collaboration on a common set of norms and rules for maritime policy.

Just as the island dispute between Japan and China has raised new questions for the alliance about the U.S. commitment to defend Japan, it has also created new political opportunity for nationalist voices. For those in Japan who seek greater military power or a more independent foreign policy from the United States, popular anxiety about Japan's security environment provides the opportunity for advocacy that would have been unthinkable a decade ago. Worries about the reliability of the United States will raise the bar on alliance reassurance, and though reassurance of U.S. support for Japan's security has long been a core task of U.S. policymakers, new and demonstrable mechanisms for integrating alliance security planning will offer a way to anchor the alliance more firmly within U.S. strategy. Instead of periodic revision of the U.S.-Japan bilateral guidelines for defense cooperation, these guidelines should be built into the regular alliance framework of security consultations and coordinated with U.S. and Japanese national defense plans. Moreover, an alliance strategy for responding to provocations short of actual war should be considered so as to develop an alliance crisis-management plan.

Finally, the United States and Japan should consider how to best incorporate the question of historical legacy into their alliance relationship. Although reconciliation is largely a task for those who were directly involved in conflict, developing a shared historical record of Asia's twentieth-century conflicts might benefit from the participation of a variety of nations, including the United States. Moreover, the U.S. role in the postwar settlement of Northeast Asia is central to the understanding of the postwar peace. Washington has not been a bystander in the postwar order in Asia, and it should not assume that role now as questions about the legitimacy of the San Francisco Peace Treaty and other regional peace treaties are called into question. New generations of Asian citizens, including Japanese, are asking new questions about the origins of the postwar peace, and the domestic politics surrounding this revisionist impulse will be important drivers of policy in Asia. U.S. policy too must include an approach to regional reconciliation, and the United States and Japan must acknowledge their continuing effort at postwar reconciliation. Reconciliation has been the cornerstone of bilateral U.S.-Japan relations for more than half a century, and the United States and Japan should not hesitate to look back at that choice. As with all reconciliation efforts, however, more can be done. A visit by the U.S. president to the sites of the atomic bombings in Japan—the cities of Hiroshima and Nagasaki—would be one way of demonstrating the continued desire for reconciliation as the premise of the alliance partnership, and would offer a powerful example for other parties in Asia struggling to overcome the politics of national identity associated with memories of twentieth-century conflict.

# Endnotes

1. Some of the leading early analyses of the DPJ's impact on foreign policy include Leif Eric-Easley, Tetsuo Kotani, and Aki Mori, "Electing a New Japanese Security Policy? Examining Foreign Policy Visions Within the Democratic Party of Japan," *Asia Policy* 9, January 2010; Daniel Sneider, "The New Asianism: Japanese Foreign Policy Under the Democratic Party of Japan," *Asia Policy* 12, July 2011; Eric Heginbotham, Ely Ratner, and Richard J. Samuels, "Tokyo's Transformation: How Japan Is Changing, and What It Means for the United States," *Foreign Affairs*, September/October 2011; and Weston S. Konishi, "From Rhetoric to Reality: Foreign-Policy Making Under the Democratic Party of Japan," Institute for Foreign Policy Analysis, April 2012.

2. For an in-depth analysis of the institutional impact of Japan's political change, see Tomohito Shinoda, *Contemporary Japanese Politics: Institutional Changes and Power Shifts* (New York: Columbia University Press, 2013).

3. In both elections, the DPJ lost the bulk of its seats, placing it on par with the newly arrived Nippon Ishin no Kai (Japan Restoration Party). In the 2012 lower house election, the DPJ lost 173 seats, dropping from 230 to 57. This put the DPJ just slightly ahead of the Japan Restoration Party, which captured 54 seats. The LDP increased its seat share by 176 seats, from 118 to 294. In the 2013 upper house election, the DPJ lost 26 seats, from 85 to 59. The Japan Restoration Party, which faced its own challenges at the time, grew only slightly, from 6 to 9 seats. The LDP, however, increased its share by 31 seats, from 84 to 115.

4. For a reflective discussion of this ambition by a former secretary-general of the DPJ, see Katsuya Okada, *Seiken kōtai: Kono kuni wo kaeru* [Change in Government: Changing This Country] (Tokyo: Kodansha, 2008).

5. The DPJ won the most seats in 2009, 308 in the lower house, compared with the LDP in 2005 (296) and 2012 (294). But the gap between the winner and the next largest party increased each year. In 2005, the LDP won 183 more seats than the DPJ. In 2009, the DPJ won 189 more than the LDP, and in 2012, the LDP won 237 more than the DPJ.

6. In 1993, as the LDP and others deliberated electoral reforms, a new umbrella coalition of reformist parties led by Morihiro Hosokawa came into power for a short-lived attempt at running the government. But the prospect for real policy change did not arrive until the newly formed DPJ won a landslide victory in the 2009 lower house election. The DPJ won 308 of 480 of seats, the largest margin of victory in postwar lower house elections.

7. Japan's seven prime ministers in the 1990s were Toshiki Kaifu (1989–91), Kiichi Miyazawa (1991–93), Morihiro Hosokawa (1993–94), Tsutomu Hata (1994), Tomiichi Murayama (1994–96), Ryutaro Hashimoto (1996–98), and Keizo Obuchi (1998–2000). The two U.S. presidents were George H.W. Bush (1989–93) and Bill Clinton (1993–2001).

8. The three LDP prime ministers were Shinzo Abe (2006–2007), Yasuo Fukuda (2007–2008), and Taro Aso (2008–2009). Prime Ministers Abe and Fukuda reshuffled the cabinet once during their respective tenures, making a total of five cabinets during the three years from 2006 to 2009.

9. The three DPJ prime ministers were Yukio Hatoyama (2009–2010), Naoto Kan (2010–2011), and Yoshihiko Noda (2011–2012).

10. Over three years at the helm of Japan's government, the DPJ had five foreign ministers—Katsuya Okada (2009–2010), Seiji Maehara (2010–2011), Yukio Edano (2011), Takeaki Matsumoto (2011), and Koichiro Genba (2011–2012)—and four defense ministers—Toshimi Kitazawa (2009–2011), Yasuo Ichikawa (2011–2012), Naoki Tanaka (2012), and Satoshi Morimoto (2012).

11. The use of censure motions in the upper house to undermine the cabinet became a regular feature of the divided Diet. The upper house had previously passed only one censure motion before 2007 (against Defense Agency director-general Fukushiro Nukaga in 1998). Although the censure motions in the upper house were nonbinding, they prevented cabinet members from speaking and thus limited their ability to advocate for government policy choices. The DPJ-controlled upper house passed censure motions against Prime Ministers Yasuo Fukuda (June 11, 2008) and Taro Aso (July 14, 2009). In both cases, no-confidence motions were easily voted down in the LDP-controlled lower house, so neither prime minister resigned immediately. Aso went on to dissolve the Diet the next week, but Fukuda did step down three months later. After the DPJ lost its majority in the upper house in 2010, the LDP successfully crippled DPJ cabinets repeatedly through the use of censure motions. Together with other opposition parties, the LDP passed censure motions against six DPJ cabinet members and one prime minister, including Chief Cabinet Secretary Yoshito Sengoku (November 26, 2010); Minister of Land, Infrastructure, and Transport Sumio Mabuchi (November 27, 2010); Defense Minister Yasuo Ichikawa (December 9, 2011); National Public Safety Commission Chairman and Minister for Consumer Affairs and Food Safety Kenji Yamaoka (December 9, 2011); Minister of Land, Infrastructure, and Transport Takeshi Maeda (April 20, 2012); Defense Minister Naoki Tanaka (April 20, 2012), and Prime Minister Yoshihiko Noda (August 29, 2012). All six of the cabinet ministers resigned their posts or were replaced in cabinet reshuffles shortly thereafter, and Prime Minister Noda dissolved the Diet and called an election in the fall of 2012. Later, after the return of the LDP, opposition parties did manage to pass a censure motion against Prime Minister Shinzo Abe on June 26, 2013, but it came just before the campaign period for the July 2013 upper house election and thus was viewed as largely symbolic. For more information on censure motions, see Sheila A. Smith, "Japan's 'New Politics': Tactics in the 'Divided Diet'," *Asia Unbound*, CFR.org, January 12, 2012, http://blogs.cfr.org/asia/2012/01/12/japan%E2%80%99s-%E2%80%9Cnew-politics%E2%80%9D-tactics-in-the-%E2%80%98divided-diet%E2%80%99.

12. Before becoming prime minister, Hatoyama published an article in the Japanese magazine *Voice* in which he wrote that globalism centered on the United States would be over in the near future ("Sofu Ichiro ni mananda 'yūai' to iu tatakai no hatajirushi" ['Fraternity': My Motto That I Learned From My Grandfather], August 10, 2009). An abbreviated version of this article was translated into English and ran not long after in the *International Herald Tribune*, raising questions in the United States about the DPJ's ultimate intentions for Japan's relationship with Washington ("A New Path for Japan," August 26, 2009). Prime Minister Junichiro Koizumi had advocated for building an East Asian community years earlier, but his concept seemed to complement the alliance relationship rather than offer an alternative to it.

13. The Hatoyama cabinet sought to address outstanding opposition in Okinawa to the
relocation of a U.S. Marine airfield from the highly populated Ginowan City to Nago
City in the north. With its coalition partners, the Japan Socialist Party (JSP) and the
People's New Party (PNP), the first DPJ government argued for a new approach, one
that relocated the marines from Okinawa to a small island in Kyushu. Ultimately,
Hatoyama failed to gain local support for his alternative plan, and quickly abandoned
his position in favor of the plan negotiated by the LDP, leading the JSP to leave the
ruling coalition and ultimately to his resignation. The DPJ elected Naoto Kan to take
his place and the new Kan cabinet endorsed the original plan to move U.S. Marine Air
Station Futenma to Nago City.

14. Ichiro Ozawa, *Blueprint for a New Japan: The Rethinking of a Nation* (Tokyo: Kodansha
International, 1994), originally published in Japanese by Kodansha in 1993.

15. Ichiro Ozawa led a series of political parties after he departed from the LDP in 1994.
After his partnership with Tsutomu Hata in the New Frontier Party dissolved, Ozawa
formed his own Liberal Party in 1998 and even joined a coalition government with
the LDP to support Keizo Obuchi as prime minister in 1999. Though some in the
LDP wanted Ozawa to return to their party, others did not, and so in 2003, before the
general election, Ozawa turned to the DPJ to form an electoral coalition. Ozawa was
elected president of the DPJ in April 2006 and led the party to upper house victory in
2007. He served as president until political scandal forced him to step down in May
2009, and Yukio Hatoyama led the DPJ to victory just months later.

16. Liberal Democratic Party of Japan, "Sangiin senkyo kōyaku 2013 (Upper House Election Manifesto 2013)," July 2013; "Jimintō seiken kōyaku" [LDP Manifesto], December
2012, https://www.jimin.jp/policy/manifest; Shigeru Ishiba, "Nihon wo, torimodosu.
Kenpō wo, torimodosu" [Restore Japan. Restore the Constitution], (Tokyo: PHP Institute, 2013).

17. Morihiro Hosokawa, "Are U.S. Troops in Japan Needed? Reforming the Alliance,"
*Foreign Affairs*, July/August 1998.

18. Liberal Democratic Party of Japan, "Nihon koku kenpō kaisei sōan" [Draft for Revision of the Constitution of Japan], April 27, 2012, https://www.jimin.jp/activity/
colum/116667.html.

19. Ministry of Foreign Affairs of Japan (MOFA), "The SACO Final Report," December
2, 1996, http://www.mofa.go.jp/region/n-america/us/security/96saco1.html.

20. National Diet of Japan, "Nihonkoku to amerika gasshūkoku to no aida no sogokyor-
yoku oyobi anzenhoshō jyōyaku dai roku jyō ni motozuku shisetsu oyobi kuiki narabini
nihonkoku ni okeru gasshūkoku guntai no chii ni kansuru kyōtei no jisshi ni tomonau
tochi tō ni kansuru tokubetsu sochi hō" [Act on Special Measures Concerning U.S.
Forces Japan's Use of Lands, Facilities, and Areas Consequent Upon Implementation of Agreement Under Article VI of the Treaty of Mutual Cooperation and Security between Japan and the United States of America, Regarding Facilities and Areas
and the Status of United States Armed Forces in Japan], originally passed May 15,
1952, amended by Law No. 39 on April 23, 1997, http://law.e-gov.go.jp/htmldata/S27/
S27HO140.html.

21. In addition to revising the Japan-U.S. Status of Forces Agreement, the DPJ's manifesto
said the party would "move in the direction of re-examining the realignment of the
U.S. military forces in Japan and the role of the U.S. military bases in Japan." Democratic Party of Japan, "Manifesto 2009," July 27, 2009, http://www.dpj.or.jp/article/
manifesto2009.

22. The DPJ's agenda, however, was predominantly domestic policy reform. Of its fifty-
five policy recommendations, only five were related to foreign policy.

23. MOFA, "United States-Japan Roadmap for Realignment Implementation," May 1, 2006, http://www.mofa.go.jp/region/n-america/us/security/scc/doc0605.html.

24. MOFA, "Agreement Between the Government of Japan and the Government of the United States of America Concerning the Implementation of the Relocation of III Marine Expeditionary Force Personnel and Their Dependents from Okinawa to Guam," February 17, 2009, http://www.mofa.go.jp/region/n-america/us/security/agree0902.pdf. http://www.mofa.go.jp/region/n-america/us/security/agree0902.pdf.

25. In his press conference afterward, Minister Kitazawa said he wanted to listen to the people (of Okinawa) firsthand and grasp the realities of the situation in Okinawa to make a sound judgment. Ministry of Defense, "Minister of Defense Kitazawa's Visit to Okinawa," *Japan Defense Focus* 15, November 2009, http://www.mod.go.jp/e/jdf/n015/leaders.html#activity03.

26. "Hatoyama's Latest Futenma Tack: Move Choppers to Tokunoshima," *Kyodo News*, April 10, 2010, available via the *Japan Times*, http://www.japantimes.co.jp/news/2010/04/10/national/hatoyamas-latest-futenma-tack-move-choppers-to-toku-noshima/#.U583FvldXzg.

27. "Hatoyama's Plan to Move Marines to Tokunoshima Gets Icy Reception," *Japan Times*, April 29, 2010, http://www.japantimes.co.jp/news/2010/04/29/national/hatoyamas-plan-to-move-marines-to-tokunoshima-gets-icy-reception/#.U582IvldXzg.

28. The two governors, Hirokazu Nakaima of Okinawa and Shigefumi Matsuzawa of Kanagawa, met with senior Defense and State Department officials as well as Senator Daniel Inouye (D-HI) and Representative Ike Skelton (D-MO) (http://www.stripes.com/news/okinawa-official-in-u-s-for-sofa-futenma-talks-1.96166). They were also invited to a roundtable discussion at the Council on Foreign Relations.

29. U.S. Embassy in Tokyo, "Joint Announcement on a Framework Regarding Environmental Stewardship at U.S. Armed Forces Facilities and Areas in Japan," December 25, 2013, http://japan.usembassy.gov/e/p/tp-20131225-01.html.

30. For the internal MOFA report, see MOFA, "Gaimushō naibu chōsa hōkokusho" [MOFA Internal Investigation Report], March 5, 2010, http://www.mofa.go.jp/mofaj/gaiko/mitsuyaku/pdfs/hokoku_naibu.pdf. For the report from the expert committee, see MOFA, "Yūshikisha iinkai ni yoru hōkokusho" [Report by the Expert Committee], March 9, 2010, http://www.mofa.go.jp/mofaj/gaiko/mitsuyaku/pdfs/hokoku_yushiki.pdf.

31. Comments by Foreign Minister Katsuya Okada, Committee on Foreign Affairs, Lower House, March 17, 2010, National Diet Library of Japan's Database System for the Minutes of the Diet, http://kokkai.ndl.go.jp.

32. U.S. Department of Defense, "Nuclear Posture Review," April 2010, http://www.defense.gov/npr/docs/2010%20nuclear%20posture%20review%20report.pdf.

33. For more information on Japan's contributions to nuclear nonproliferation, see Nobumasa Akiyama, "The Compliance Structure of the Nuclear Non-Proliferation Regime and Japan's Non-Proliferation Policy Assets," *Hitotsubashi Journal of Law and Politics* 41

34. Sheila A. Smith, "Japan's Iran Sanctions Dilemma," *Asia Unbound*, CFR.org, January 31, 2012, http://blogs.cfr.org/asia/2012/01/31/japan%E2%80%99s-iran-sanctions-dilemma/.

35. MOFA , "Additional Accompanying Measures Pursuant to United Nations Security Council Resolution on Iran," December 9, 2011, http://www.mofa.go.jp/announce/announce/2011/12/1209_02.html; "Additional Accompanying Measures Pursuant to United Nations Security Council Resolution on Iran," March 13, 2012, http://www.mofa.go.jp/announce/announce/2012/3/0313_01.html.

36. The Self-Defense Force (SDF) is split into three branches: the Maritime Self-Defense Force (MSDF), Ground Self-Defense Force (GSDF), and Air Self-Defense Force

(ASDF). When the SDF is operating as a coalition force alongside other nations, it is sometimes referred to as the "JSDF" for "Japan Self-Defense Force." However, the most commonly used acronym when referring to Japan's military is "SDF," which will be used in this report.

37. MOFA , "Japan's Contribution to United Nations Peacekeeping Operations," 2014, http://www.mofa.go.jp/policy/un/pko/pdfs/contribution.pdf.

38. Ministry of Defense, "Haichi haken kokusai kyūentai: katsudō shūryō" [The End of Activities of the International Relief Team Dispatched to Haiti], http://www.mod.go.jp/js/Activity/Pko/pko_minustah.htm; Ministry of Defense, "Minami Sūdan haken shisetsutai no katsudō" [Activities of SDF Engineering Team Dispatched to South Sudan], http://www.mod.go.jp/js/Activity/Pko/pko_unmiss.htm.

39. From 2001 to 2007, the MSDF refueled ships 794 times. From 2008 to 2010, it did so 145 times. Ministry of Defense, "'Tero tono tatakai' to jieitai no katsudō" [The Fight Against Terrorism and the SDF's Activities], September 2007, http://www.shindo.gr.jp/magazine/article/0138-071015_01.swf; Ministry of Defense, "Defense of Japan 2010." For a map of where the MSDF undertook refueling missions, see Ministry of Defense, "Indoyō ni okeru hokyū shien katsudō" [Refueling Operations in the Indian Ocean], http://www.mod.go.jp/js/Activity/Past/oef.htm.

40. See testimony by Akihisa Nagashima, Special Meeting on Anti-Terrorism, Lower House, October 17, 2008; comments by Akihisa Nagashima, Committee on National Security, Lower House, November 27, 2008, National Diet Library of Japan's Database System for the Minutes of the Diet, http://kokkai.ndl.go.jp.

41. On hearing Nagashima's proposal in favor of antipiracy operations in the Gulf of Aden, Prime Minister Aso replied, "*Jimintō no kata ga teian sareteirunoka to omotta gurai desu. Socchokuna tokoro wo iimasukeredomo*" [Frankly speaking, I feel as if this proposal was made by the LDP]. Remarks by Prime Minister Taro Aso and Representative Akihisa Nagashima, Special Committee on Counterterrorism and Japan's Logistics and Humanitarian Support for Iraq, Lower House, October 17, 2008.

42. Remarks by Representative Akihisa Nagashima, Committee on National Security, Japan House of Representatives, November 27, 2008. Nagashima went on to serve as Prime Minister Noda's policy adviser and authored a book on Japan's alliance management. Akihisa Nagashima, *Katsubei to iu ryūgi gaikō anzenhoshō no riarizumu* [The Way to Utilize the United States: Realism in Diplomacy and Security], (Tokyo: Kodansha Ltd., October 2013).

43. The advisory committee was chaired by Shigetaka Sato, chief executive officer of Keihan Electric Railway Co., Ltd. Prime Minister's Office, "Japan's Visions for Future Security and Defense Capabilities in the New Era: Toward a Peace-Creating Nation," Council on Security and Defense Capabilities in the New Era, August 2010, http://www.kantei.go.jp/jp/singi/shin-ampobouei2010/houkokusyo_e.pdf.

44. Ministry of Defense, "National Defense Program Guidelines for FY2011 and Beyond," December 17, 2010, http://www.mod.go.jp/e/d_act/d_policy/pdf/guidelinesFY2011.pdf; Ministry of Defense, "Mid-Term Defense Program (FY2011–2015)," December 17, 2010, http://www.mod.go.jp/e/d_act/d_policy/pdf/mid_termFY2011-15.pdf.

45. For more information on the origins of the 2010 NDPG, see Noboru Yamaguchi, "Deciphering the New National Defense Program Guidelines," Tokyo Foundation, March 24, 2011, http://www.tokyofoundation.org/en/articles/2010/deciphering-the-new-national-defense-program-guidelines-of-japan.

46. The DPJ established the Government Revitalization Unit in September 2009 to review administrative projects within each ministry and find areas where the budget could be reduced. The party also held highly popularized, televised hearings where

senior bureaucratic officials would defend their ministry's expenditures. Democratic Party of Japan, "The DPJ's Track Record in the Fields of Eliminating Wasteful Spending and Regional Revitalization," December 3, 2012, http://www.dpj.or.jp/english/news/?num=20588.

47. In terms of actual expenditures, Japan's defense budget in FY2009, the year the DPJ came into office, was 4.70 trillion yen. For the next three years, defense expenditures declined annually by 0.4 percent, spending in FY2010 at 4.68 trillion yen, in FY2011 at 4.62 trillion yen, and in FY2012 at 4.65 trillion yen. In his first year in office, FY2013, Prime Minister Abe raised defense spending by 0.8 percent, to 4.68 trillion yen, back to the FY2010 level. In absolute terms, defense spending for FY2010–2012 was the lowest since 1993. Japan's Longterm Statistics, "Bōei kankei hi (Defense-Related Budget)," http://www.stat.go.jp/data/chouki/31.htm; Ministry of Defense, "Bōei kankei hi to sono suii" [Changes in Japan's Defense-Related Budget], *Defense of Japan 2013*, chapter 4, section 2.

48. MOFA , "Agreement Between Japan and the United States of America Concerning New Special Measures Relating to Article XXIV of the Agreement Under Article VI of the Treaty of Mutual Security and Cooperation Between Japan and the United States of America, Regarding Facilities and Areas and the Status of United States Armed Forces in Japan," January 21, 2011, http://www.mofa.go.jp/region/n-america/us/security/pdfs/agree1101.pdf.

49. For more information on U.S.-Japan cooperation following the March 11 triple disasters, see Michael J. Green and Kiyoaki Aburaki, "Partnership for Recovery and a Stronger Future," Center for Strategic and International Studies Task Force in Partnership with Keidanren, November 2011, http://csis.org/publication/partnership-recovery-and-stronger-future. For a careful assessment of Japan's policymaking during and after the Great East Japan Earthquake, see Richard J. Samuels, *3.11: Disaster and Change in Japan* (Ithaca, NY: Cornell University Press, 2013).

50. Andrew Feickert and Emma Chanlett-Avery, "Japan 2011 Earthquake: U.S. Department of Defense (DOD) Response," June 2, 2011, p. 1, http://www.fas.org/sgp/crs/row/R41690.pdf.

51. In the wake of the Fukushima Daiichi nuclear disaster, three committees were set up to independently investigate the accident: the Investigation Committee on the Accident at the Fukushima Nuclear Power Stations of Tokyo Electric Power Company, established by the Kan cabinet on May 24, 2011; the Fukushima Nuclear Accident Independent Investigation Commission, established by the National Diet of Japan on December 8, 2011; and the Independent Investigation Commission on the Fukushima Nuclear Accident, established by Yoichi Funabashi and the Rebuild Japan Initiative Foundation in September 2011. For the final reports of the three investigations, see Investigation Committee on the Accident at the Fukushima Nuclear Power Stations of Tokyo Electric Power Company, Cabinet Office of Japan, Yotaro Hatamura (chairman), "Final Report of the Investigation Committee on the Accident at the Fukushima Nuclear Power Stations of Tokyo Electric Power Company," July 23, 2012, http://www.cas.go.jp/jp/seisaku/icanps/eng/final-report.html; Fukushima Nuclear Accident Independent Investigation Commission, National Diet of Japan, Kiyoshi Kurosawa (chairman), "The Official Report of the Fukushima Nuclear Accident Independent Investigation Commission," July 5, 2012, http://warp.da.ndl.go.jp/info:ndljp/pid/3856371/naiic.go.jp/en; Independent Investigation Commission on the Fukushima Nuclear Accident, Rebuild Japan Initiative Foundation, Koichi Kitazawa (chairman), "The Fukushima Daiichi Nuclear Power Station Disaster: Investigating the Myth and Reality," March 2012, http://rebuildjpn.org/en/project/fukushima/report/. http://rebuildjpn.org/en/project/fukushima/report.

52. Prime Minister's Office, "Address by H.E. Dr. Yukio Hatoyama Prime Minister of Japan at the Sixty-Fourth Session of the General Assembly of the United Nations," September 24, 2009, http://japan.kantei.go.jp/hatoyama/statement/200909/ehat_0924c_e.html.

53. Prime Minister's Office, "Address by H.E. Dr. Yukio Hatoyama Prime Minister of Japan: Japan's Commitment to Asia: Toward the Realization of an East Asian Community," November 15, 2009, http://japan.kantei.go.jp/hatoyama/statement/200911/15singapore_e.html.

54. MOFA, "Statement by the Chief Cabinet Secretary Yohei Kono on the Result of the Study on the Issue of 'Comfort Women'," August 4, 1993, http://www.mofa.go.jp/policy/women/fund/state9308.html.

55. MOFA, Statement by Prime Minister Tomiichi Murayama, "On the Occasion of the 50th Anniversary of the War's End," August 15, 1995, http://www.mofa.go.jp/announce/press/pm/murayama/9508.html.

56. Prime Minister Kan offered his "deep remorse and heartfelt apology" to South Korea in a speech marking the one hundredth anniversary of Japan's annexation of the Korean peninsula. Prime Minister's Office, "Statement by Prime Minister Naoto Kan," August 10, 2010, http://japan.kantei.go.jp/kan/statement/201008/10danwa_e.html.

57. Comments by Prime Minister Yoshihiko Noda, Budget Committee, House of Councillors, August 27, 2012, National Diet Library of Japan's Database System for the Minutes of the Diet, http://kokkai.ndl.go.jp.

58. Heritage Foundation, "The U.S.-Japan Alliance and the Debate Over Japan's Role in Asia," speech by Governor of Tokyo Shintaro Ishihara, April 16, 2012, http://www.heritage.org/events/2012/04/shintaro-ishihara.

59. "Japan Is Back" speech by Shinzo Abe, given at the Center for Strategic and International Studies, "Statesmen's Forum: HE Shinzo Abe, Prime Minister of Japan," February 22, 2013, http://csis.org/event/statesmens-forum-he-shinzo-abe-prime-minister-japan.

60. National Diet of Japan, "Kokka anzenhoshō kaigi secchi hō" [Act for Establishment of the National Security Council], originally passed May 27, 1986 (No. 71), amended December 4, 2013 (No. 89); National Diet of Japan, "Tokutei himitsu no hogo ni kansuru hōritsu" [Act on Protection of Specified Secrets], passed December 13, 2013 (No. 108); National Security Council of Japan, "National Security Strategy," December 17, 2013, http://www.mod.go.jp/j/approach/agenda/guideline/pdf/security_strategy_e.pdf; Ministry of Defense, "National Defense Program Guidelines for FY2014 and Beyond," December 17, 2013, http://www.mod.go.jp/j/approach/agenda/guideline/2014/pdf/20131217_e2.pdf; Ministry of Defense, "Medium Term Defense Program (FY2014–FY2018)," December 17, 2013, http://www.mod.go.jp/j/approach/agenda/guideline/2014/pdf/Defense_Program.pdf.

61. U.S. Department of Defense, "Joint Statement of the Security Consultative Committee: Toward a More Robust Alliance and Greater Shared Responsibilities," October 3, 2013, http://www.defense.gov/pubs/U.S.-Japan-Joint-Statement-of-the-Security-Consultative-Committee.pdf.

62. MOFA, "The Guidelines for Japan-U.S. Defense Cooperation," September 23, 1997, http://www.mofa.go.jp/region/n-america/us/security/guideline2.html.

63. The 1997 guidelines discussions opened the way for the passage of emergency mobilization laws in Japan in 2003 and 2004 that outlined the legal basis for responding to an attack on Japan. Three laws, including the Armed Attack Situation Response Law, were enacted in 2003. Seven additional laws, including the Law Concerning the Measures for Protection of the Civilian Population in Armed Attack Situations,

were enacted in 2004. MOFA, "Framework for Responses to Armed Attack Situation and Other Situations," *Defense of Japan 2006*, chapter 2, section 3, http://www.mod.go.jp/e/publ/w_paper/2006.html. The current discussions on the constitution and the Japanese government's interpretation of the right of collective self-defense are also expected to allow the Japanese SDF to act in concert with U.S. forces to defend Japan's security. The Advisory Panel on Reconstruction of the Legal Basis of Security, "Report of the Advisory Panel on Reconstruction of the Legal Basis of Security," May 15, 2014, http://www.kantei.go.jp/jp/singi/anzenhosyou2/dai7/houkoku_en.pdf; Prime Minister's Office, "Press Conference by Prime Minister Abe," May 15, 2014, http://japan.kantei.go.jp/96_abe/statement/201405/0515kaiken.html.

64. See Ministry of Economy, Trade, and Industry, "Bōei sōbi iten sangensoku wo sakuteishimashita" [Decision Made on Three Principles on the Control of Arms Exports], April 1, 2014, http://www.meti.go.jp/press/2014/04/20140401001/20140401001.pdf; Ministry of Defense, "Three Principles on Transfer of Defense Equipment and Technology, April 1, 2014, http://www.mod.go.jp/e/pressrele/2014/140401_02.pdf; Ministry of Defense, "Implementation Guidelines for the Three Principles on Transfer of Defense Equipment and Technology," April 1, 2014, http://www.mod.go.jp/e/pressrele/2014/140401_01.pdf.

65. For example, see MOFA, "5th Japan-Australia 2+2 Foreign and Defense Ministerial Consultations: Joint Press Release," June 11, 2014; MOFA. http://www.mofa.go.jp/mofaj/files/000041606.pdf; "Japan-India Summit Meeting," January 25, 2014, http://www.mofa.go.jp/s_sa/sw/in/page3e_000138.html; the International Institute for Strategic Studies, "Advancing Military-to-Military Cooperation: Itsunori Onodera," Shangri-La Dialogue, May 31, 2014, http://www.iiss.org/en/events/shangri%20la%20dialogue/archive/2014-c20c/plenary-2-cb2e/itsunori-odonera-be7d.

66. Ministry of National Defense, People's Republic of China, "Announcement of the Aircraft Identification Rules for the East China Sea Air Defense Identification Zone of the P.R.C.," November 23, 2013, http://eng.mod.gov.cn/Press/2013-11/23/content_4476143.htm.

67. The ASDF scrambled 38 times against Chinese aircraft in fiscal 2009, 96 times in fiscal 2010, 156 times in fiscal 2011, 306 times in fiscal 2012, and 415 times in fiscal 2013. Fiscal 2013 also marked the first year that scrambles against Chinese aircraft exceeded those against Russian aircraft (359 times). Joint Staff, Ministry of Defense, "Heisei 25-nendo no kinkyū hasshin jisshi jyōkyō ni tsuite" [Status of Scrambles in Fiscal Year 2013], April 9, 2014, http://www.mod.go.jp/js/Press/press2014/press_pdf/p20140409.pdf; Ministry of Defense, "Press Conference by the Defense Minister Onodera," May 25, 2014, http://www.mod.go.jp/e/pressconf/2014/05/140525.html; "Extra Press Conference by the Defense Minister Onodera," June 11, 2014, http://www.mod.go.jp/e/pressconf/2014/06/140611.html.

68. In his joint press conference with Prime Minister Abe, President Obama said, "Let me reiterate that our treaty commitment to Japan is absolute, and Article 5 covers all territories under Japan's administration, including the Senkaku Islands." White House, "Joint Press Conference with President Obama and Prime Minister Abe of Japan," April 24, 2014, http://www.whitehouse.gov/the-press-office/2014/04/24/joint-press-conference-president-obama-and-prime-minister-abe-japan.

69. Speaking at the Yokota Air Base in Japan, Hagel said that the aim of his trip was to "reassure our allies, our partners here in this part of the world of our commitment, our continued commitment, to our partnership, our friends, and our treaty obligations. We're serious about that, as you all know now." U.S. Department of Defense, Remarks by Secretary Hagel at a Troop Event at Yokota Air Base, Japan, April 5, 2014,

http://www.defense.gov/Transcripts/Transcript.aspx?TranscriptID=5406. Later that week in Beijing, Hagel spoke before the PLA National Defense University and said, "The United States has been clear about the East and South China Sea disputes. We do not take a position on the sovereignty claims, but we expect these disputes to be managed and resolved peacefully and diplomatically, and oppose the use of force or coercion. And our commitment to the region is unwavering." U.S. Department of Defense, "Secretary of Defense Speech: PLA National Defense University," April 8, 2014, http://www.defense.gov/Speeches/Speech.aspx?SpeechID=1838.

70. U.S. Department of State, "Maritime Disputes in East Asia," Testimony by Assistant Secretary of State for East Asian and Pacific Affairs Daniel R. Russel, House Committee on Foreign Affairs, Subcommittee on Asia and the Pacific, February 5, 2014, http://www.state.gov/p/eap/rls/rm/2014/02/221293.htm.

71. Park Geun-hye, "A Plan for Peace in North Asia," *Wall Street Journal*, November 12, 2012.

72. In his first press conferences as chief cabinet secretary, Suga was asked by reporters about the Abe cabinet's stance on both the Murayama and Kono Statements. Suga said that the Abe cabinet would continue to uphold the Murayama Statement. However, in the case of the Kono Statement, Suga emphasized that this should not be a political or diplomatic issue, and that it was instead a matter for experts and historians to decide. He did not comment on whether the Abe government would continue to uphold the statement. Prime Minister's Office, "Press Conference by the Chief Cabinet Secretary (AM)," December 27, 2012, http://japan.kantei.go.jp/tyoukanpress/201212/27_a.html; "Press Conference by the Chief Cabinet Secretary (PM)," December 27, 2012, http://japan.kantei.go.jp/tyoukanpress/201212/27_p.html. The question about whether the Abe government would revise the Kono Statement resurfaced after Suga mentioned in the Diet that the government had created an expert committee to examine the drafting of the Kono Statement. In his daily press conference on March 3, Suga responded to questions from reporters by saying that the Abe government would uphold the Kono Statement. He reiterated this stance on March 10. Prime Minister's Office, "Press Conference by the Chief Cabinet Secretary (PM)," March 3, 2014, http://japan.kantei.go.jp/tyoukanpress/201403/03_p.html; "Press Conference by the Chief Cabinet Secretary (AM)," March 11, 2014, http://japan.kantei.go.jp/tyoukanpress/201403/1204275_9550.html. The March 10 press conference is available online only in Japanese. However, Suga was asked on March 11 about his statements the previous day, and this transcript is available in English.

73. In an interview with the *Sankei Shimbun* shortly after his election, Prime Minister Abe said that he hoped to release a "forward-oriented" statement in addition to the 1995 Murayama Statement. He also said that his government would review the 1993 Kono Statement (*Sankei Shimbun*, December 31, 2012). In February 2013, Prime Minister Abe appeared before the upper house and reiterated that in addition to upholding the core of the Murayama Statement, he would like to issue his own forward-oriented statement, as Prime Minister Koizumi had done during his tenure. Comments by Prime Minister Shinzo Abe, Upper House Plenary Session, February 1, 2013. For the Koizumi Statement, see MOFA, "Statement by Prime Minister Junichiro Koizumi," August 15, 2005, http://www.mofa.go.jp/announce/announce/2005/8/0815.html.

74. The Cabinet Office of Japan asked two questions: whether respondents viewed the current state of Japan-Korea relations as good, and whether respondents held positive feelings (*shinkinkan*) toward South Korea. In both polls, Japanese attitudes toward Korea took a sharp dive beginning in 2012. The number who thought Japan-Korea relations were good dropped from 58.5 percent in 2011 to 18.4 percent in 2012 and 21.1 percent in 2013, the lowest levels since the Cabinet Office began asking this question in 1986. In terms of Japanese sentiments toward South Korea, the number who had positive feelings fell from 62.2 percent in 2011 to 39.2 percent in 2012 and 40.7 percent

in 2013, the steepest decline since the Cabinet Office first asked this question in 1978. Cabinet Office of Japan, "Gaikō ni kansuru yoron chōsa" [Survey on Foreign Policy], survey conducted October 2013, published November 25, 2013, http://www8.cao.go.jp/survey/h25/h25-gaiko/index.html.

75. Comments by Prime Minister Shinzo Abe, National Diet of Japan, Budget Committee, Japan House of Representatives, March 5, 2007. On February 20, 2014, Representative Hiroshi Yamada of the Japan Restoration Party expressed his doubts about the validity of the Kono Statement, and asked Chief Cabinet Secretary Suga to have the government reexamine the Kono Statement. On February 28, Suga replied in the Diet that the Abe cabinet had formed an expert team to undertake the reexamination. Although Yamada asked Suga to verify what the comfort women victims had said, Suga replied that this would be impossible as the Japanese government at the time did not collect any evidence to confirm the victims' testimonies. On May 29, Suga said that the government would issue a report for the lower house budget committee before the end of the current Diet session in June. Comments by Hiroshi Yamada and Yoshihide Suga, Budget Committee, Lower House, February 20, February 28, and May 28, 2014.

76. Remarks by Prime Minister Shinzo Abe, Budget Committee, Upper House, March 14, 2014.

77. The report was drafted by the Study Team on the Details Leading to the Drafting of the Kono Statement. The five-member study group was chaired by Keiichi Tadaki, lawyer and former prosecutor-general, and also included Hiroko Akizuki, professor, Faculty of International Relations, Asia University; Makiko Arima, journalist and former direct of the Asian Women's Fund; Mariko Kawano, professor, Faculty of Law, Waseda University; and Ikuhiko Hata, modern historian. For the official report, see Prime Minister's Office, "Details of Exchanges Between Japan and the Republic of Korea (ROK) Regarding the Comfort Women Issue: From the Drafting of the Kono Statement to the Asian Women's Fund," June 20, 2014, http://japan.kantei.go.jp/96_abe/documents/2014/__icsFiles/afieldfile/2014/06/20/JPN_ROK_EXCHANGE.pdf. Chief Cabinet Secretary Suga explained the conclusions of the policy review in a press conference. Prime Minister's Office, "Press Conference by the Chief Cabinet Secretary (PM)," June 20, 2014, http://www.kantei.go.jp/jp/tyoukanpress/201406/20_p.html.

78. U.S. Embassy in Tokyo, "Statement on Prime Minister Abe's December 26 Visit to Yasukuni Shrine," December 26, 2013, http://japan.usembassy.gov/e/p/tp-20131226-01.html.

79. Sheila A. Smith, "President Obama and Japan-South Korean Relations," *Asan Forum*, March 25, 2014, http://www.theasanforum.org/president-obama-and-japan-south-korean-relations.

80. Tomohito Shinoda, *Koizumi Diplomacy* (Seattle: University of Washington Press, 2007).

81. *Yomiuri Shimbun*, September 6, 2005.

82. *Sankei Shimbun*, October 30, 2001; *Yomiuri Shimbun*, October 30, 2001; *Yomiuri Shimbun*, January 30, 2002.

83. NHK News, August 26, 2009; *Yomiuri Shimbun*, October 26, 2009; *Nikkei Shimbun*, January 6, 2010.

84. Hitoshi Tanaka, "Hatoyama's Resignation and Japan's Foreign Policy," Japan Center for International Exchange, *East Asia Insights* 5, no. 3, June 2010, http://www.jcie.or.jp/insights/5-3.html.

85. Once out of office, Hatoyama returned to Okinawa and argued that his claim as prime minister about the need for the base was "politically expedient," revealing the inconsistency of his stance on the base relocation plan. *Okinawa Times*, February 13, 2011.

86. See, for example, Yuichi Hosoya, "Inertia and Drive in the DPJ's Security Policy," Nippon.com, July 5, 2012, http://www.nippon.com/en/currents/d00039/.

87. Sheila A. Smith, "Japan and the East China Sea Dispute," *Orbis*, Summer 2012.

88. Managing transitions in the U.S. government has proven difficult for foreign policy-making, and the impact is discussed in Kurt Campbell and James Steinberg's book on transitions. Kurt M. Campbell and James B. Steinberg, *Difficult Transitions: Foreign Policy Troubles at the Outset of Presidential Power* (Washington, DC: Brookings Institution Press, 2008).

89. For more information on U.S. bases in Asia, see Sheila A. Smith, "Shifting Terrain: The Domestic Politics of the U.S. Military Presence in Asia," East-West Center Special Reports No. 8, March 2006.

90. Yoichi Funabashi, *Alliance Adrift* (New York: Council on Foreign Relations Press, 1999), originally published in Japanese by Iwanami Shoten in 1997.

91. Sheila A. Smith, "A Sino-Japanese Clash in the East China Sea," Contingency Planning Memorandum No. 18, Council on Foreign Relations Press, April 2013, http://www.cfr.org/japan/sino-japanese-clash-east-china-sea/p30504.

# About the Author

**Sheila A. Smith** is senior fellow for Japan studies at the Council on Foreign Relations. Smith joined CFR from the East-West Center in 2007, where she specialized in Asia-Pacific international relations and U.S. policy toward Asia. From 2004 to 2007, she directed a multinational research team in a cross-national study of the domestic politics of the U.S. military presence in Japan, South Korea, and the Philippines. Prior to joining the East-West Center, Smith was on the faculty of the Department of International Relations at Boston University and on the staff of the Social Science Research Council. She has been a visiting researcher at the Japan Institute of International Affairs and the Research Institute for Peace and Security, and at the University of Tokyo, University of the Ryukyus, and Keio University. She is vice chair of the U.S.-Japan Conference on Cultural and Educational Exchange (CULCON), a binational advisory panel of government officials and private sector members. Her publications include *Shifting Terrain: The Domestic Politics of the U.S. Military in Asia* and *Local Voices, National Issues: Local Initiative in Japanese Policymaking*. Smith's newest book, *Intimate Rivals: Japanese Domestic Politics and a Rising China*, will be available from Columbia University Press in 2015. She earned her BA and PhD degrees from the department of political science at Columbia University.

# Japan's Political Transition and the U.S-Japan Alliance Roundtables

"The Rise of China and Japan's Strategic Adjustment," with Masafumi Ishii, Ambassador of Policy Planning and International Security Policy, Ministry of Foreign Affairs (January 26, 2011)

"Rethinking Japan's China Strategy," with Hitoshi Tanaka, Chairman, Institute for International Strategy, the Japan Research Institute, Ltd., and Senior Fellow, Japan Center for International Exchange (January 31, 2011)

"A Conversation with Ambassador John V. Roos,"Ambassador Extraordinary and Plenipotentiary, Embassy of the United States in Japan (June 7, 2011)

"A Conversation with Kurt M. Campbell," Assistant Secretary of State for East Asian and Pacific Affairs (November 22, 2011)

"A Conversation with J. Thomas Schieffer," former U.S. Ambassador to Japan (January 12, 2012)

"A Conversation with Yoichi Funabashi," President of the Rebuild Japan Initiative Foundation (March 27, 2012)

"Update on Japan's Foreign Policy," with Hideki Asari, Deputy Director, Japan Institute of International Affairs (JIIA); Tsutomu Kikuchi, Professor, Aoyama Gakuin University; Daisaku Ikejima, Professor, Waseda University; Toshihiro Nakayama, Professor, Aoyama Gakuin University; and Asuka Matsumoto, Research Fellow, JIIA (May 9, 2012)

"Political Leadership in Japan and U.S.-Japan Relations," with Jun Saito, Chief Executive Officer, Logos Education Group; and Yuka Uchida, former Public Policy Scholar, Woodrow Wilson International Center for Scholars (September 26, 2012)

"From LDP to DPJ to LDP Again?," with Tomohito Shinoda, Professor, Research Institute, International University of Japan (November 2, 2012)

"A Conversation with Joseph S. Nye," University Distinguished Service Professor and former Dean, Harvard Kennedy School (November 30, 2012)

"A Conversation with Yukio Okamoto," President, Okamoto Associates, Inc. (January 25, 2013)

"A Conversation with Gerald Curtis," Burgess Professor of Political Science, Columbia University, and former Director of Columbia University's Weatherhead East Asian Institute (April 29, 2013)

"A Conversation on Sino-Japanese Relations," with Ryosei Kokubun, President, National Defense Academy of Japan; and Noboru Yamaguchi, Lieutenant General (retired), Japan Ground Self-Defense Force, and Professor, National Defense Academy of Japan (September 18, 2013)

"Japan's Postelection Priorities," with Kenichiro Sasae, Ambassador of Japan to the United States (September 20, 2013)

"U.S. Alliances in Northeast Asia," with James P. Zumwalt, Deputy Assistant Secretary of State for East Asian and Pacific Affairs; and Amy E. Searight, Principal Director for East Asia, Office of the Secretary of Defense (September 27, 2013)

"Japan's Political Change and Alliance Management," with Kazuyoshi Umemoto, Ambassador, Permanent Mission of Japan to the United Nations (December 9, 2013)

"Historical Perceptions and U.S.-Japan Relations," with Toshihiro Nakayama, Professor, Aoyama Gakuin University; and Nobumasa Akiyama, Professor, Hitotsubashi University (December 16, 2013)

"Japan-Korea Relations and East Asian Security," with Yoshihide Soeya, Director, Institute of East Asian Studies and Professor, Keio University (January 24, 2014)

Council on Foreign Relations

58 East 68th Street
New York, NY 10065
tel  212.434.9400
fax 212.434.9800

1777 F Street, NW
Washington, DC 20006
tel  202.509.8400
fax 202.509.8490

*www.cfr.org*